HARD PLASTIC DOLLS, II

Identification and Price Guide
by Polly and Pam Judd

Jill by Vogue Dolls, Inc: pop-up advertiseme[...]
(see page 228).

Acknowledgements

Many people from all over the United States have helped mold this book. Their inquiries and contributions have helped us add to the original *Hard Plastic Dolls* book. We wish to thank all of the people who spoke to us as we traveled, sent us letters, and offered ideas and encouragement. It is great fun to be associated with all the "doll" people.

Our special thanks and appreciation to Mr. Richard Sherin, Chief Museum Conservator of the Strong Museum in Rochester, New York, for his help with the conservation of hard plastic dolls.

Mr. H.B. Samuels, of the Reliable Toy Co., helped us with the Coronation Section.

Vivien Brady-Ashley, Sandra Crane, Marianne Gardner, Marge Meisinger and Nancy Roeder were very helpful with Alexander pictures and information.

Mary Elizabeth Poole really helped start this book with her wonderful suggestions and boxes of research.

Dorothy Hesner, one of the first collectors of hard plastic dolls, could remember the "Good Old Days."

The Cleveland Doll Club always encouraged us and gave us support when we needed it.

The following people contributed pictures, information and ideas: Barbara Andresen, Phyllis Appell, Patricia Arches, Mary Ann Bauman, Ester Borgis, Laura May Brown, Beatrice Campbell, Nancy Carlton, Ruth Casey, Nancy Catlin, Barbara Comienski, Athena Crowley, Mary Jane Cultrona, Kathryn Davis, Sherri Dempsey, Jean Dicus, Sharlene Doyle, Diane Hoffman, Kathy George, Sally Herbst, Dorothy Hesner, Virginia Ann Heyerdahl, Jill Kaar, Helen Keefe, Eunice Kier, Chree Kysar, Lois Janner, Arline Last, Diane Loney, Christine Lorman, Kim Lusk, Margaret Mandel, Glenn Mandeville, Elizabeth Martz, Ruth Moss, Shirley Niziolek, Roslyn Nigoff, Elsie Ogden, Pat Parton, Thelma Purvis, Louise Schnell, Lois Seketa, Betty Shriver, Carmen Smotherman, Sandra Strater, Elaine Timm, Pat Timmons, Mary Ann Watkins and Gigi Williams.

We also wish to thank our editor, Donna H. Felger, and the entire staff of Hobby House Press, Inc.

Additional Copies of this book may be purchased at $12.95
from
HOBBY HOUSE PRESS, INC.
900 Frederick Street
Cumberland, Maryland 21502
or from your favorite bookstore or dealer.
Please add $2.25 per copy postage.

ISBN: 0-87588-343-5

Table Of Contents

Preface

Our first book, *Hard Plastic Dolls*, was a beginning in the identification of hard plastic dolls. Since it was intended to be a small paperback handbook that could easily be carried and stored, it was necessarily limited in scope. In the second book we have added a number of companies and dolls which were not in book one.

The following dolls are included in this book:
1. All-hard plastic
2. Dolls with vinyl heads and hard plastic bodies
3. Baby dolls with hard plastic heads and cloth, latex and rubber bodies

Hard Plastic Dolls, I covered 84 companies. This was by far the majority of the companies which made hard plastic dolls. *Hard Plastic Dolls, II* will add other manufacturers and concentrate on companies which did not have as many pictures and information as in the first book.

Foreign hard plastic dolls are very interesting and collectible. They are now appearing more and more in the American market. Individual companies and countries have different and unusual hard plastic material. Some of it appears to be celluloid which is the original base of the hard plastic material developed during World War II. While different, these dolls are beautiful and very collectible.

Since the identification of clothes is very important to collectors of these dolls, there will be even more space given to company brochures, catalogs and advertisements of the fashions of that period than in the first book.

There is a section of suggestions for the conservation of doll clothing from the hard plastic era.

There are additions to the identification features found at the end of the first book. For the most part, the authors have not repeated these identification tips. For more complete details, please consult the section at the end of *Hard Plastic Dolls, I*.

One special addition to the Identification Section is research of the small *Ginny*-type and "Chubby-type" dolls which were so popular. Pictures of their bodies have been included for easy reference. This has been requested by many of our readers.

For ease of identification and understanding, this book will have the same general format as *Hard Plastic Dolls I* and have many cross references. The abbreviation "HP" means hard plastic and will be used throughout the book.

Finally, at the back of this book there will be a price update of the dolls in *Hard Plastic Dolls, I* which have seemed to have changed in value. Prices of the dolls in this book will continue to appear under the picture.

The Beginning of Hard Plastic Dolls

The very tiny doll in *Illustration 1* belongs to Dorothy Hesner of Cicero, Illinois. Her mother had a little gift and embroidery store in Chicago during World War II. About 1943 or 1944 she began selling these tiny hard plastic dolls. During the war toys were scarce, and Dorothy repainted hundreds of these for her mother who put them in pretty card boxes along with fabric, scissors, needles and thread and sold them for sewing kits. Dorothy dressed this doll in a Girl Scout uniform, and she still has it today.

Plastic was used in the various services during the war. Wally Judd, our husband and father, was a soldier in the U.S. Air Force in Alaska. He repaired airplanes using plastic, and he made a beautiful small hard plastic locket for Polly and sent it to her. Someway this substance found its way into civilian life during the war years and into the lives of the happy children who lived near the little gift shop in Chicago.

Kimport reported in their *Doll Talk* magazine in January-February of 1974 that the first real plastic doll was put out by Ideal Novelty Company in 1940 but was discontinued after about a year due to war restrictions on materials. The body and legs were in one piece. The arms were movable and all of it was a radically different texture that looked and felt like human flesh. It could be pinched, wrinkled and became warm to the touch. The heads were made of hard plastic and the bodies were kapoc stuffed. It was a great success but the fortunes of war prevented it from continuing on to become a very profitable commercial enterprise.

However, it was a beginning. Today, as the 20th century draws to a close, we look back on that early era and to the very first hard plastic dolls and remember how beautiful they were.

Illustration 1. Tiny HP doll costumed by Dorothy Hesner. *Dorothy Hesner Collection.*

In 1946 the Sears catalog showed many of the composition dolls which were quickly manufactured for children who had not had many dolls during World War II. While a few of their other baby dolls had hard plastic heads, Sears proudly presented a baby doll and toddler, "For the first time! Made entirely of Plastic." This doll, made by Ideal, still has original clothes and is in the collection of Mary Elizabeth Poole.
SEE: *Illustration 2. Mary Elizabeth Poole Collection.*

First All-Hard Plastic Doll Offered by Sears: 15in (38cm); toddler and 14in (36cm) baby; advertised as having lifelike hands and feet; separate fingers and toes; molded, tinted hair; sleep eyes with real lashes; dressed in sunsuits in assorted colors, styles, materials; 1946.
This doll was made by Ideal.
SEE: *Illustration 3.* 1946 Sears Christmas catalog. *Barbara Andresen Collection.*

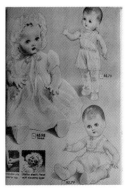

1.   2.   3.

How To Use This Book

This book is set up in the same format as *Hard Plastic Dolls, I*. There are several ways to use this book depending upon the reader's knowledge of a doll. If the doll is marked and you know the company name, turn immediately to the company section and look up the company name which appears in alphabetical order. You will find a list of dolls and their characteristics, dates of production if possible and a current price range.

If the doll is marked but you do not know the company name (example "R & B"), turn to the Doll Marks Guide on page 233. You will find these letters indicate the Arranbee Company. Then turn to the Arranbee section for pictures and more references. Most marked hard plastic dolls have their numbers, letters and symbols listed in the Doll Marks Guide. This is one of the few parts of the Doll Identification Guide of *Hard Plastic Dolls, I* which is repeated in this book.

If the doll is unmarked or if the mark is not listed, turn to the Doll Identification Guide. There, at the beginning of the section you will find another Table of Contents listing the various doll characteristics which will help you. Examples are arm hooks, eyes and fasteners. There are many others. In this section the doll features will help you narrow the possibilities and refer you back to the doll company. Often there will be references to the page numbers of specific identification details in *Hard Plastic Dolls, I*. The authors have tried not to duplicate the information unless it is very important.

When you have exhausted these options and still have not identified your doll, there is an excellent section "Differences Among Hard Plastic, Composition and Vinyl Dolls" in *Hard Plastic Dolls, I*. This will help you determine if your doll is hard plastic.

The authors are very appreciative and thankful to the many, many people who took the time to write to us about their dolls and send us new information and wonderful pictures. This book is really the result of their efforts.

The abbreviation "HP" for hard plastic has been used throughout this book.

System Used For Pricing Dolls

Prices in this book reflect a range of prices from various parts of the United States. These prices are given for the specific dolls photographed. Unless otherwise noted, these dolls would be in excellent to mint condition and include original clothes. There would be higher prices for a doll with an original box, tag and/or "tissue" mint conditions. Local prices will vary. It is also very true that what is eagerly sought in one section of the country will sell sluggishly in another location.

Dolls that were presumed to be rare have a way of appearing after a book is published showing their pictures and listing their prices. When this happens, collectors and dealers will have to adjust to a downward scale.

Because clothes were important to society in the 1950s, these dolls often had elegant and lovely clothes. Even everyday clothes were fancy and surprisingly well made. As with all dolls, unusual clothes will add to the quoted prices. Modern undressed dolls are usually worth 1/4th to 1/3rd the value of a doll in original clothes.

Doll Conservation

by Richard W. Sherin

Authors' Note: Richard W. Sherin is Chief Museum Conservator at the Strong Museum in Rochester, New York. The Strong Museum's collection of some 20,000 dolls is the most comprehensive in any museum. Before assuming his present position, Mr. Sherin was Assistant Conservator of Decorative Arts and Furniture at the Indianapolis Museum of Art. He holds a Master of Arts degree in the Conservation of Historic and Artistic Works from Cooperstown (NY) Graduate Program.

If at all possible, store your doll collection in a cool, dry and clean environment. Higher temperatures accelerate unwanted chemical reactions and lead to the more rapid deterioration of both a doll and its accessories. Relative humidity control is also very necessary and often critical. Maintain the relative humidity as close as you can to 50 percent year round. Avoid attics and cellars.

As a general rule, it is better to store a doll and its original box separately. These boxes usually are of poor quality; they are often highly acidic and can be very damaging when direct contact is permitted between the doll and the box. The best solution is to store the doll by itself in an archival box of appropriate dimension. Padding it with neutral tissue paper will help secure the doll's position. Store clothing and other accessories in a second box, taking care to wrap each piece with the same inert tissue. If the doll must remain in its original box, use tissue or two-ply acid-free matt board to isolate it (from the material[s] of the box) the best way you can. Do not use any tapes or glues for this; simply wrap or cut-and-fit dry.

Dolls in storage should be regularly inspected to guarantee their well-being. Reorient and repack the dolls where appropriate in order to minimize creasing of clothing fabrics and to maintain the proper form.

The nature of the lighting under which dolls are displayed is also very critical for optimum preservation. Generally, two types of (light) sources are commonly employed — incandescent (regular light bulbs) and fluorescent (tubes). Both can be used, but be aware that the latter emits considerable ultraviolet (UV) radiation. Very high in energy, UV causes severe damage to organic materials (textiles, wood, paper, etc.) in the form of embrittlement, fading, shrinkage, and discoloration. If fluorescent tubes are used, make sure to also install UV-filtering plastic sleeves over each one. These can be purchased from a reliable lighting firm and their use will eliminate over 95 percent of this very harmful energy. Whatever your light source, the level of visible light at the doll should not exceed five (5) footcandles. A dimmer switch is the easiest solution here. Even then the exposure should be limited as much as possible.

A Note About Plastics

by Richard W. Sherin

All plastics are polymers. Basically, they consist of many small units (called monomers) which have been linked together chemically. In addition, they can contain a number of other materials to give them color and other desirable physical properties. Research has shown that most types are susceptible to deterioration caused by oxygen and ultraviolet radiation. While we can't eliminate oxygen very readily, we can, as described above, minimize exposure to UV. Some plastics are created by the addition of water molecules; as they age, they can lose this water and therefore become a different material with very different properties. About this we can do little. Others, such as polyvinylchloride (PVC), turn yellow as they age and give off hydrochloric acid (HCl). This acid could be potentially harmful to susceptible materials nearby. Celluloid (cellulose nitrate) plastics — Kewpie dolls are an example — are especially sensitive to alkaline materials. Celluloid is also flammable and can self-destruct, giving off nitric acid HNO_3...again potentially destructive to nearby materials. Early forms of celluloid may smell of oils such as camphor, added initially as a plasticizer but which (eventually) made the celluloid harder, and somewhat less flammable.

Any odor associated with plastic has to be due either to some incomplete curing process or to some form of decomposition. Research into the deterioration mechanisms of plastics is still in its infancy. Only recently have conservators recognized the types of problems peculiar to plastics and begun to seek appropriate remedies (if any exist). An improperly chosen solvent or cleaning solution may activate an odor by partly dissolving the surface. The novice should seek expert advice before attempting any cleaning beyond water and should take the time to carefully record any observations for collective benefit.

While it appears that much plastic deterioration is inherent and inevitable, we can still slow it down somewhat by following some of the preceding suggestions.

A & H Doll Mfg. Corp.

The registered trademarks, the trademarks and the copyrights appearing in italics within this chapter belong to A & H Doll Mfg. Corp.

A & H Doll Mfg. Corp. had one of the most innovative and comprehensive doll lines in the hard plastic era. The dolls were popularly priced and designed to appeal to many different types of customers. The dolls themselves were rarely marked but were usually well tagged.

Today they are not the most expensive of collectible dolls but if the dolls are found mint-in-box and tagged, they are pretty and appealing. They also document the entire period of hard plastic dolls.

Dolls of Destiny: Advertisement from *McCall's Needlework*, Fall-Winter 1953-1954. These dolls were one of the first hard plastic dolls to be authentically dressed in historical costumes. An innovation at the time, they were expensive ($8.95) and came in a beautiful blue brocade box. The costumes were lovely and well made. Each doll carried her own storybook written by a well-known children's author and historian. The dolls are (a) *Mary Todd Lincoln*, (b) *Marie Antoinette*, (c) *Elizabeth Woodville Grey*, (d) *Martha Washington*, (e) *Queen Isabella*, (f) *Betsy Ross*, (g) *Queen Elizabeth I*, (h) *Empress Josephine*, (i) *Empress Eugenie*, (j) *Molly Pitcher*, (k) *Priscilla Alden* and (l) *Queen Victoria*. (For general characteristics, see *Illustration 5*.)

In 1953 hard plastic dolls were new and the cost was high. Today these same "Dolls of Destiny" are considered to be one of the less expensive collectible dolls. However, the costumes are unusual and made with attention to detail.

MARKS: "Pat's Pending" (back); "Doll of Destiny and name of doll" (dress tag)
SEE: *Illustration 4. McCall's Needlework*, Fall-Winter 1953-1954.
PRICE: $35-45

4. a   b   c   d   e   f   g   h   i   j   k   l

5.

6.

Dolls of Destiny *Molly Pitcher* (right) HP: 12in (31cm); head turning walker; jointed at neck, arms and legs; molded shoes with bow (see Identification Guide, *Hard Plastic I*, page 283A); closed mouth; 2nd and 3rd fingers on each hand molded together; two dimples on each knee; sleep eyes; molded lashes; black, white and yellow colonial style dress with green striped underskirt; white hat, collar, apron; carries a copper pitcher which was made in Italy; 1953-1954.

> **MARKS:** "A Doll of Destiny//Molly Pitcher//1754-1832" (dress tag) "Pat's Pending" (back)
> **SEE:** *Illustration 5.*
> **PRICE:** $35-45

Dolls of Destiny *Priscilla* (left): HP; 12in (31cm); gray rayon dress and cape; white apron and bonnet; 1953-1954.

> **MARKS:** "Doll of Destiny// Priscilla//1604-1680" (dress tag) "Pat's Pending" (back)
> **SEE:** *Illustration 5.*
> **PRICE:** $35-45

Dolls of Destiny *Betsy Ross* (right): HP; 12in (31cm); (see *Illustration 5* for general characteristics); 1953-1954.
There were at least two different materials used for the dresses of *Betsy Ross*. Both were green to follow the famous painting which was used in many schoolbooks. The picture was painted by Charles Weisgerber and exhibited at the Columbian Exposition in Chicago in 1893. The *Betsy* on the right has the book which was included with each doll. She has a pair of toy scissors hanging at her waist.

> **MARKS:** "Doll of Destiny//Betsy Ross 1752-1836" (dress tag of both dolls); "Pat's Pending" (back)
> **SEE:** *Illustration 6.*
> **PRICE:** $35-45

7.

George Washington: HP; 8in (20cm); green velvet coat; maroon pants with gold braid; white lace jabot; tricorn hat; white wig; circa early 1950s.

 MARKS: None (doll); "A Marcie Doll" (box)
 SEE: *Illustration 7.*
 PRICE: $10-12

8.

Gigi Identification: (see also Identification Guide, page 237).

 This doll came in at least three forms:
 1. An early all-HP hip pin straight leg walker
 2. A later all-HP with regular walking mechanism and bent knees
 3. Vinyl head doll with HP body and regular walking mechanism with bent knees and rooted hair

 The skin color is a light, clear flesh tone with a lovely natural type coloring; the eyebrows are delicately painted; the sleep eyes have molded lashes; deep red coloring on tiny lips; standard arm hooks (see *Hard Plastic Dolls, I*, page 264I); molded ear stands away from body toward the back of the head; head turning walker; no dimples above fingers; dimples above toes; two lines above ankles on bent knee model; good detail on fingernails and toenails; large navel.

Gigi: HP; 8in (20cm); dressed in outfit seen in brochure on page 3, No. 8; red print jumper with rickrack and lace trim; matching bonnet; "Rau Sklikits" on inside of snap.

 MARKS: None (doll)
 SEE: *Illustration 8.*
 PRICE: $25-35

Gigi: HP; 7½in (19cm) head-turning walking doll; standard arm hook (see Identification Guide, *Hard Plastic Dolls, I*, page 265K); 2nd and 3rd fingers molded together; straight legs; two lines under knees; two dimples behind knees; finely sculptured toes with two dimples over them; no dimples on hands; black and white striped skirt with pink felt top and two embroidered black crosses; lace on sleeves; No. 709; (for picture of body, see Identification Guide, page 237); mid 1950s.

 MARKS: None (doll)
 SEE: *Illustration 9. Pat Parton Collection.*
 PRICE: $25-35

9.

11

Gigi Brochure: HP; 8in (20cm); (for general characteristics, see page 11); head turning walker; hair may be set; circa 1955.

No. 7240—DRESSED DOLL
No. 724—OUTFIT ONLY
Lipstick Red and White Furry Trimmed skating costume with White Boots and Ice Skates.

★ A *Gigi* DOLL ★

GIGI DOLL OUTFITS
may be purchased Separately
*No. 729—Leatherette Sport Jacket outfit only.
*No. 730—Rain Outfit Only
*No. 7300—Dressed Doll in Rain Outfit
*Not illustrated

No. 725—OUTFIT ONLY
A real fur coat fully lined, with a matching hat and muff.

★ A *Gigi* DOLL ★

No. 7260—DRESSED DOLL
No. 726—OUTFIT ONLY
An exquisite formal gown of taffeta threaded with gold with a darling net stole to match.

8 Inch Dress-up Dolls

Gigi ©

DOLLS & OUTFITS

DRESSED DOLL **$1⁹⁸**

OUTFIT ONLY **$1⁰⁰**

"*Gigi*" and her Custom Made Outfits are sold at leading department and toy stores everywhere. Fine dressmaker detail with handy snaps for easy changes. Choose from the widest selection of dainty clothes suitable for every occasion.

Each and every outfit is a rare delight . . . expertly made to the last detail. You'll love making Gigi your best dressed doll.

MANUFACTURED BY
A & H DOLL MFG. CORP.
WOODSIDE 77, N. Y.

MY NAME IS

Gigi ©

White and gold Majorette Costume with Boots and Baton to lead the parade.

No. 7200
Dressed Doll
No. 720
Outfit Only

I WALK - I SIT - I SLEEP
I TURN MY HEAD
YOU CAN SET MY HAIR
AND CHANGE MY CLOTHES

10.

No. 7010—DRESSED DOLL
No. 701—OUTFIT ONLY
A dainty pastelle organdy skirt with felt top, natural straw up-turned hat to complete outfit.

★ A *Gigi* DOLL ★

No. 7020—DRESSED DOLL
No. 702—OUTFIT ONLY
Luscious pink or aqua organdy dress with matching bonnet and purse.

No. 7030—DRESSED DOLL
No. 703—OUTFIT ONLY
Little people cotton print with contrasting color chintz apron and adorable straw bonnet.

★ A *Gigi* DOLL ★

No. 7040—DRESSED DOLL
No. 704—OUTFIT ONLY
Cherry red dress, lace trimmed, with darling little apron and black straw hat.

No. 7270—DRESSED DOLL
No. 727—OUTFIT ONLY
Blue denim jeans with a red and white checked blazer, up-turned hat and glasses.

★ A *Gigi* DOLL ★

No. 7280—DRESSED DOLL
No. 728—OUTFIT ONLY
Davy Crockett Outfit, suede fringed jacket and shirt. Leatherette brown belt, rifle and shoulder sling with real fur-tailed cap.

No. 7050—DRESSED DOLL
No. 705—OUTFIT ONLY
Rose print dress trimmed with pink with adorable pink bonnet to match.

★ A *Gigi* DOLL ★

No. 7060—DRESSED DOLL
No. 706—OUTFIT ONLY
Black and white striped taffeta skirt and lace trimmed felt top, black straw hat.

11.

12

No. 7070—DRESSED DOLL
No. 707—OUTFIT ONLY
Black and white gibson dress with belt and sailor straw hat.

No. 7090—DRESSED DOLL
No. 709—OUTFIT ONLY
Adorable guimpe dress, striped skirt and net sleeves and black straw hat.

No. 7110—DRESSED DOLL
No. 711—OUTFIT ONLY
Tiny print yellow dress with charming yellow apron and fashionable black straw hat.

No. 7130—DRESSED DOLL
No. 713—OUTFIT ONLY
Smart Navy Blue hat and coat trimmed with white collar and cuffs and white matching purse.

★ A *Gigi* DOLL ★   ★ A *Gigi* DOLL ★   ★ A *Gigi* DOLL ★   ★ A *Gigi* DOLL ★

No. 7080—DRESSED DOLL
No. 708—OUTFIT ONLY
Pink checked sun dress with white pique jacket, with darling natural straw hat.

No. 7100—DRESSED DOLL
No. 710—OUTFIT ONLY
Orange dress with smart forest green jacket and matching hat.

No. 7120—DRESSED DOLL
No. 712—OUTFIT ONLY
Gold matelasse lounging set. smart contrasting trousers with gold slippers.

No. 7140—DRESSED DOLL
No. 714—OUTFIT ONLY
A delightful rickrack trimmed cotton print dotted with lace and matching hat.

12.

No. 7150—DRESSED DOLL
No. 715—OUTFIT ONLY
Tiny red print on white cotton, sweet little apron with beautiful blue ribbon bow for hair.

No. 7170—DRESSED DOLL
No. 717—OUTFIT ONLY
Charming cotton print trimmed with velvet and lace and natural straw hat.

No. 7190—DRESSED DOLL
No. 719—OUTFIT ONLY
Complete Nurse's costume with cute little cape and Nurse's cap.

No. 7220—DRESSED DOLL
No. 722—OUTFIT ONLY
Yellow and Red Cowgirl Costume complete with Vest, Hat and Boots.

★ A *Gigi* DOLL ★   ★ A *Gigi* DOLL ★   ★ A *Gigi* DOLL ★   ★ A *Gigi* DOLL ★

No. 7160—DRESSED DOLL
No. 716—OUTFIT ONLY
Highly styled tiny polka dot cotton with flower trimmed felt cloche.

No. 7180—DRESSED DOLL
No. 718—OUTFIT ONLY
Delightful school dress trimmed with velvet with perky straw hat.

No. 7210—DRESSED DOLL
No. 721—OUTFIT ONLY
Beach Costume with fashionable knit top and Hat to Match.

No. 7230—DRESSED DOLL
No. 723—OUTFIT ONLY
Gold and White Fluffy Ballet Costume and adorable little Crown on head.

13.

14.

Gigi and Revolving Carousel Wardrobe: HP with vinyl head; 8in (20cm); (for other general characteristics, see page 11); plastic carousel is transparent; holds new couturier wardrobe for 1957.

Lil' Sister with Carousel Wardrobe: all-vinyl baby doll; winks, coos, sleeps, wets, drinks; 1957.

SEE: *Illustration 14. Playthings*, March 1957.

PRICE: $25-35 (*Gigi*)
$10-15 (*Lil' Sister*)

15.

Hits for '58: advertisement in *Playthings*, February 1958.

As late as 1958 A & H was advertising some hard plastic dolls complete with doll wardrobes.

SEE: *Illustration 15.*

Prize Packages: A & H was one of the early companies to make hard plastic dolls for the mass market. Like similar companies, they were still making the popular inexpensive "fashion" dolls into the 1960s. They featured *Belles in Bells, Teens in Bells, Gigi in Bells, Lil' Sister in Bells, Belles of Nations* and other famous dolls.

MARKS: None (doll); "A & H Dolls" (engraved on bottom of bell)
SEE: *Illustration 16. Playthings*, March 1962.
PRICE: $20-25 (in bell)

16.

14

Dutch Girl in Bell: HP; 8in (20cm); sleep eyes; blonde wig; high-heeled shoes with hole in the bottom of the shoes; jointed at neck, shoulders, hips; dressed in Dutch costume with purple skirt; white dotted swiss top; felt Dutch cap; one of *Belles of Nations*; 1962.

This doll has high-heeled shoes like the doll in the "Unknown" section of *Hard Plastic Dolls, I* (see *Illustrations 519* and *520*, page 234).

> **MARKS:** None (doll); "A & H Dolls" (engraved on bottom of bell)
> **SEE:** *Illustration 17.*
> **PRICE:** $20-25

17.

Birthstone Dolls: This is an advertisement for 9in (22cm) dolls called *Birthstone Belles:*

1.	January	Garnet	7.	July	Ruby
2.	February	Amethyst	8.	August	Sardonyx
3.	March	Aquamarine	9.	September	Sapphire
4.	April	Diamond	10.	October	Opal
5.	May	Emerald	11.	November	Topaz
6.	June	Pearl	12.	December	Turquoise

> **SEE:** *Illustration 18. Playthings*, March 1962.
> **PRICE:** $10-12 each

18.

Costume Styled for *Julie* Walking Doll: boxed "Czech" outfit made for *Julie* and all 8in (20cm) walking dolls; beautiful red print skirt with black felt vest; white organdy blouse trimmed with lace; traditional Czech lace headpiece with multi-colored ribbon streamers; gripper snap says "RAU SKLIKITS" on inner part of snap; circa 1955-1957.

MARKS: "Styled for Julie//Czech//A & H Mfg. Corp."
SEE: *Illustration 19. Pat Parton Collection.*
PRICE: $5-7

19.

Active Doll Corporation

The registered trademarks, the trademarks and the copyrights appearing in italics within this chapter belong to Active Doll Corporation.

Scotch Lassie: HP; 7in (18cm); sleep eyes with lashes painted above eyes; painted-on shoes (see Identification Guide, *Hard Plastic Dolls, I,* page 285H); blonde hair; Scotch plaid skirt with red and gold ribbon top. Other dolls in the series included *American Bride, French Miss, Greek Miss, Swedish Lass, Brazil Miss, Dutch Miss, Irish Lass, German Miss, Spanish Senorita, Italian Miss, British Princess;* circa 1955.

MARKS: None (doll); "Active Doll Corporation//'I am one of the beautiful Dolls of Many Lands' " (box)
SEE: *Illustration 20.*
PRICE: $6-10

20.

Admiration Doll Company

This company made an inexpensive line of dolls which they advertised in *Playthings* in the early 1960s. Their hard plastic was a light hollow material that was used in these later dolls. They also made vinyl high-heeled dolls. There was a minimum of sewing in their costuming.

21.

Girl: inexpensive HP; 7½in (19cm); *Ginger* characteristics unless otherwise noted (see Identification Guide, *Illustration 238*); pink wig; large sleep eyes (see Identification Guide, *Illustration 246*); heavy eyebrows; unusual curves in arms; non-walker; original clothes still stapled on doll; green polka dot top; pink, green and black skirt; white paint over exposed toes to imitate shoes; *Ginger* arm hook (see *Hard Plastic Dolls, I*, page 266N); circa 1962-1965. This doll is similar to the Midwestern *Mary Jean* (page 150) but it does not have the *Mary Jean* arm hooks.

MARKS: "Admiration//Toy Co.//A1 75//Made in Hong Kong" (back)
SEE: *Illustration 21. Barbara Comienski Collection.*
PRICE: $6-10

Alden's

The Alden mail order catalog was used extensively during the hard plastic era. They advertised many dolls from known companies. They also had a line of dolls made exclusively for them.

Lil Megotoo: HP with vinyl head; 8in (20cm); walker; doll cost 88 cents; each outfit also cost 88 cents; outfits included bride dress; travel suit; majorette costume with baton; fall coat; roller skate outfit with skates; Red Cross nurse outfit; chemise dress; tea party dress; 1958.
Information came from advertisement from Davison's Store of Atlanta, Georgia, November 9, 1958.
This doll was also sold through the Alden's catalog.

22.

SEE: *Illustration 22.*
PRICE: $10-15

Alexander Doll Company, Inc.

The registered trademarks, the trademarks and the copyrights appearing in italics within this chapter belong to the Alexander Doll Company, Inc., unless otherwise noted.

In 1946 the Alexander Doll Company resumed production of their composition dolls, but very quickly turned to the new hard plastic material. By 1948 they were using hard plastic for many dolls including *Babs Ice Skater* (see *Hard Plastic Dolls, I*, page 115), *Alice in Wonderland* (see *Hard Plastic Dolls, I*, page 22), *McGuffey Ana* (see *Hard Plastic Dolls, I*, page 20), *Margaret O'Brien, Little Women* and others. They continued to use the *Margaret* face and introduced a new charmer named *Maggie*. Most of these dolls were not marked. However, their clothes were usually labeled.

The early hard plastic dolls had a deep flesh color painted on their bodies. This can be seen at the arm and leg joints. Their costumes were made of cottons, organdies, net and other materials of the period. Even today, many of these dolls still retain the transitional "quiet glow." Collectors today eagerly seek these early dolls.

Using the new innovations in plastic and cloth, by 1951 Madame Alexander's dolls had become the pace-setter of the 1950s, and she became a leader in both the doll and fashion industries.

23.

24.

Bride: HP; 14in (36cm); fully jointed; lovely red hair with soft curls; white organza over taffeta dress; long tulle veil edged with lace; tiny stiff cap with flowers at each side; green foil wrist tag with "Madame Alexander" on it; circa 1948 or 1949. Many of these early hard plastic Alexander dolls were not marked with the company name. Usually the dress was tagged.

    MARKS: "Madame Alexander" (dress tag)

    SEE: *Illustration 23. Sandra Crane Collection.*

    PRICE: $325-400 (more for larger doll)

Ringbearer: HP; 12in (31cm); toddler; fully-jointed; blonde wig over molded hair; sleep eyes; wearing white satin suit; pillow carries wedding ring; early gold cloverleaf tag; circa 1948-1950. This unusual doll is sometimes called *Precious* or *Lovey Dovey*. He was also sold with just his molded hair and no wig.

    MARKS: "Alexander" (head)

    SEE: *Illustration 24. Nancy Roeder Collection.*

    PRICE: $500-600

Knuckle-head Nellie: HP; 14in (36cm); red caracul wig; original white organdy over a satin dress; trimmed with bows; 1950. Madame Alexander often advertised on the back cover of *Playthings* and this picture was on the back cover of the May 1950 issue. The advertisement says, "...Inspired by Mary Martin's great performance in 'SOUTH PACIFIC'." In the lower right hand corner is a picture of Madame Alexander in a locket. Many of the advertisements from this period showed this locket.

   SEE: *Illustration 25. Playthings,* May 1950.
   PRICE: $600-700

25.

Cinderella: painted HP; 15in (38cm); jointed at neck, shoulders, hips; *Margaret* face; dressed in long blue satin gown with side panniers; trimmed in silver braid; silver necklace and bracelet; clothes all original; blonde formal wig with chignon held with net and jeweled gold headpiece; glass slippers; 1950. The skin color of this doll has not faded. The satin dress has retained its blue color. This is very unusual because the blue often turns to a pink or lavender shade. It has been preserved well.

   MARKS: None (doll); "Madame Alexander//New York//All Rights Reserved" (tag)
   SEE: *Illustration 26.* (Color Section, page 40).
   PRICE: $600-700 in this condition; less if fading has taken place

Pink Bride: early HP with beautiful skin tone; 14in (36cm); blonde mohair wig in original set; sleep eyes; pink satin dress with scoop neck and lace ruffle; high-necked net inset with net sleeves attached; pink net veil over a flower headpiece; pink slip and panties; nylon stockings; pink leather slippers with tiny bow; bouquet of pink flowers with matching floorline drop ribbons; all original; circa 1950. Around 1950 fashion-conscious brides could choose pink as a bridal color. While it was fashionable, it never became very popular. Madame Alexander, always a fashion leader, followed the trend and made this unusual pink bride doll.

   MARKS: None; very few of these early *Margaret*-faced dolls were marked.
   "Madame//Alexander//New York, N.Y. U.S.A." (tag on dress)
   SEE: *Illustration 27.* (Color Section, page 95).
   PRICE: $500-600+ (rare doll — very few sample prices)

19

Early Hard Plastic Portrait Dolls

At the beginning of the 1950s Madame Alexander designed a set of wonderful Pre-Portrait dolls which carried the Fashion Award label. These were done in the manner of some of the composition 21in (53cm) dolls with theatrical makeup and costumes. Six have so far been identified.

1. A bride which has come to be known as the *Victorian Bride*. So far these dolls have not been found in an Alexander box with a name on the label.
2. A lovely girl known as the so-called *Kathryn Grayson* doll. She, too, has not been found in a labeled box.
3. The *Champs-Elysees* is known as the "Lady with the Rhinestone Teardrop," and is dressed in a wonderful black lace dress over pink satin. She has been found in a labeled box.
4. A theatrical ballerina has been found in a box, and she has the name *Deborah*.
5. A beautiful doll, dressed in the manner of a Godey Lady, has been found in a box with the name *Judy* on it.
6. *Pink Champagne* is the name given to a wonderful red-headed doll according to the label on her box.

In the past few years these dolls have emerged in the same gowns in several areas of the United States. All of the dolls have clothes with fancy costume jewels and spangles handsewn in the theatrical way. Some have tags in the dresses. Others do not. Madame Alexander's design is elegant and the sewing is done in true couturier fashion.

Champs-Elysees (also known as the Lady with the Rhinestone Beauty Mark): HP; 21in (53cm); added eyelashes; blonde wig with bangs; tight strapless pink satin underdress; black lace over black tulle overdress; jeweled bracelets on both arms; black lace headpiece; round gold Fashion Academy Award tag; 1951. 1951 was the first year that Madame Alexander received the Fashion Award Gold Medal. She also received the medal in 1952, 1953 and 1954.

SEE: *Illustration 28* (Color section, page 33). *Vivian Brady-Ashley Collection.*

PRICE: (rare doll — very few samples prices)

28.

Victorian Bride: HP; 21in (53cm); *Margaret* face; normal eyelashes; dress in 3 sections; lacy net blouse that ties at waist; lined white satin bodice; draped satin skirt; five-section bustle; deep lace ruffle at bottom of skirt; lace veil formed like mantilla over stiffened bandeau; white flowers at each side of head; bouquet of white flowers in lace circle with narrow satin streamers; bodice has square snaps; skirt has round snaps; circa 1951.
MARKS: "Madame Alexander" embroidered cursive-type writing (tag)
SEE: *Illustration 29* (Color section, page 34). *Sandra Crane Collection.*
PRICE: (rare doll — very few sample prices)

Judy (also known as the Godey Lady): HP; 21in (53cm); blonde off-the-face wig; Godey period costume; white lace three-quarter top; very wide pink taffeta ruffles which sweep around the front and are caught up at the waist in back; ribbon and flower-trimmed straw hat; 1951.
SEE: *Illustration 30* (Color Section, page 35). *Diane Hoffman Collection.*
PRICE: (rare doll — very few sample prices)

Pink Champagne: HP; 21in (53cm); red wig with beautiful hair set; purple silk organza dress with underskirt; taffeta slip-pantie; decorated with beautiful multi-colored flowers and rhinestones down the right front of her dress; flowers are also on her left shoulder; pearl necklace and earrings; her loose chignon is held by a hairnet studded with "diamonds;" circa 1951. The lovely doll was found in a box labeled "Pink Champagne."
SEE: *Illustration 31* (Color section, page 36). *Vivien Brady-Ashley Collection.*
PRICE: (rare doll — very few sample prices)

Deborah Ballerina: HP; 21in (53cm); *Margaret* face; set of false eyelashes over their normal lashes (when lost it is possible to see a heavily painted line on lid); brows painted with short strokes; full lips; elaborate chignon; painted fingernails; original clothes in two pieces; white satin bodice with neckline of tulle; lace skirt over tulle underskirt which is embroidered with rhinestones and pearls; satin panties with ruffled tulle; rhinestone and pearl choker necklace; round snaps; circa 1951.
SEE: *Illustration 32* (Color Section, page 37). *Sandra Crane Collection.*
PRICE: (rare doll — very few sample prices)

Kathryn Grayson (so called): HP; 21in (53cm); *Margaret* face; dark makeup; full lips; heavy eyelashes; dress with tulle skirt and lace bodice with rhinestones; teardrop earrings; ornate necklace; flowers on each side of head; 1951.
SEE: *Illustration 33* (Color Section, page 38). *Sandra Crane Collection.*
PRICE: (rare doll — very few sample prices)

34.

35.

36.

Kathy: HP; 15in (38cm); red pigtail wig; *Maggie* face; fully jointed; red and black pedal pushers; red corduroy weskit; white organdy blouse; black velvet cap with red feather; watch fob; roller skates; brown tie shoes; box for curlers; circa, 1951. *Kathy* was also made in 18in (46cm) and 23in (58cm) sizes. Another roller skating costume is a blue cotton knit one-piece body suit and a full circle skirt of pink gabardine. F.A.O. Schwarz pictured a blue two-toned dress with rickrack trim in their 1951 catalog.

> MARKS: Fashion Academy Award tag; brochure with "Kathy" on cover
> SEE: *Illustration 34. Nancy Roeder Collection.*
> PRICE: $400-425

Maggie: HP; 14in (36cm); see *Hard Plastic Dolls, I* for general characteristics; unusual black pigtail wig; not a walker; Fashion Award sticker on bottom of the box; red dress with white organdy pinafore; circa 1951-1952.

> SEE: *Illustration 35. Marianne Gardner Collection.*
> PRICE: $375-425

Wendy Bride (doll on left): HP; 15in (38cm); walker; white taffeta long dress with white tulle overskirt; long tulle veil topped by lace bonnet; white bridal bouquet; long nylon stockings; satin shoes; *Maggie* face; 1953.

> SEE: *Illustration 36* (doll on left). *Marianne Gardner Collection.*
> PRICE: $340-370

Rosamund (doll on right): HP; 15in (41cm); long yellow taffeta bridesmaid dress with yellow tulle overskirt; originally she carried a hat box with curlers; doll was inspired by the book *Rosamund* by Maria Edgeworth; *Maggie* face: 1953. The doll also came in an 18in (46cm) size. The dress came in other pastel colors also.

   SEE: *Illustration 36* (doll on right). *Marianne Gardner Collection.*

   PRICE: $340-370 15in (41cm)
   $425-475 18in (46cm)

37.

Annabelle: HP; 15in (38cm); *Maggie* face; shown in 1952 F.A.O. Schwarz catalog; inspired by Kate Smith's stories of Annabelle; 1952.

   SEE: *Illustration 37. Playthings,* August 1952.

   PRICE: $400-425

Tommy Bangs: HP; 15in (38cm); all original light pants with dark blue coat with double set of buttons; pink shirt; from Louisa M. Alcott's book *Little Men*; 1952 only.

Other dolls in the series in 1952 include *Stuffy* and *Nat.*

   See: *Illustration 38. Marianne Gardner Collection.*

   PRICE: $700-750+

38.

Stuffy: HP; 14in (33cm); *Maggie* face; blue, white and black checked pants; blue jacket and cap; from Louisa M. Alcott's book *Little Men*; all original except tie is missing; 1952 only.

   MARKS: "Stuffy//Madame Alexander//New York U.S.A." (dress tag)

   SEE: *Illustration 39. Patricia Arches Collection.*

   PRICE: $700-750+

39.

Glamour Girls: HP; 18in (46cm); used both *Maggie* and *Margaret* faces; seven different dolls; walking mechanism; each doll has a hat box and curlers; all the dresses are from the 1860s with full skirts and hoops; made for one year only, 1953.

1. Below *Blue Danube*: blue cotton print with pink and white flowers; black trim and ribbons; lace trim around neck and on puffed sleeves; stiff white lace bonnet. SEE: *Illustration 40. Nancy Roeder Collection.*
2. Not pictured *Edwardian*: blonde wig; black taffeta and lace hat with pink ostrich feather; pink embossed cotton gown; black lace gloves.
3. Not pictured *Victorian*: formal pink taffeta gown; black velvet bodice; full skirt has a garland of pink roses; black and pink velvet ribbons trim outfit; black straw lace bonnet with pink rosebuds; tulle bow.
4. Not pictured *Godey Lady*: red taffeta gown and bonnet; gray fur cloth stole; red hatbox.
5. Not pictured *Civil War*: white taffeta dress; wide red sash; tiny red rosebuds and green leaves sewn on front of gown; white horse hair braid picture hat.
6. Not pictured *Queen Elizabeth II*: court gown of white brocade and blue Sash of Garter; jeweled coronet, earrings and bracelet; long white gloves.
7. *Picnic Day*: (See *Illustration 41*.)
   PRICE: $600-800 each

40.

Glamour Girl: HP; 18in (46cm); walking mechanism; hat box and curlers; dressed in *Picnic Day*; strawberry pink dress with green leaves; wide green sash; trimmed with black val lace; large straw hat with pink rosebuds; 1953.

SEE: *Illustration 41. Vivian Brady Ashley Collection.*

PRICE: $600-800

41.

24

Elaine of the Me and My Shadow Series: HP; 18in (46cm); portrait dolls; matching 7½in (19cm) miniature portrait dolls; garden party blue organdy dress trimmed with many rows of tiny val lace ruffles and stitching. The underdress is pink taffeta. There is a white taffeta hoop skirt and matching panties. The dress has puff sleeves, a round neck outlined with pearls and a big blue satin sash. There is a picture hat of white straw lace and pink satin slippers. 1954.

SEE: *Illustration 42. Sandra Crane Collection.*
PRICE: $600-800

The other dolls in the "Me and My Shadow Series" include:
1. *Mary Louise:* (See *Hard Plastic Dolls I,* page 26.)
2. *Blue Danube Waltz:* soft blue taffeta dance dress with side drapery of blue and gold striped taffeta; elaborate hairdo with a tiny gold coronet; gold necklace and jeweled bracelets (not pictured).
3. *Queen Elizabeth:* ornate white court gown with blue sash of the Order of the Garter; star and white orlon ermine cape; jeweled tiara, earrings and bracelet; long white gloves (not pictured).
4. *Cherie:* bouffant opera gown of heavy white satin gracefully draped with white roses; Goya pink taffeta opera coat is lined and fastened at the neck with a big bow; satin bag and the hairdress are rose trimmed (not pictured).
5. *Agatha:* iridescent taffeta Edwardian gown trimmed with delicate braid, flowers and pleated tulle; tight basque ends in a drapery which falls in a short train in back; ornate necklace; trimmed hat; white kid gloves; parasol (not pictured).

Victoria of Me and My Shadow Series: HP; 18in (46cm); 1850s costume; slate blue taffeta with side panniers and bustle drapery; narrow white silk braid; small hat of starched white lace with topknot of roses and forget-me-nots; fuchsia ribbons; fuchsia velvet reticule; 1954.

SEE: *Illustration 43. Vivien Brady-Ashley Collection.*
PRICE: $600-800

42.   43.

Binnie Walker: HP; 15in (38cm); clothes in suitcase include gabardine coat, matching pillbox hat, white gloves, muff of pretend leopard, tartan school dress, nightgown, playsuit, blouse, pedal pushers, bonnet, shoes, socks, curlers for her Saran wig; head turning walker; sleep eyes; 1954.

> SEE: *Illustration 44.* Marshall Field & Co. 1954 Christmas catalog. *Barbara Andresen Collection.*
> PRICE: $500-600+

Binnie doll in a suitcase is all set for the Grand Tour. There's an impressive list of things to take packed in her cardboard suitcase. She's dressed for travel in her organdy dress with panties and net trimmed half slip, short socks and black slippers. She's stowed away a rayon gabardine coat, matching pillbox hat, little white gloves and muff of pretend-leopard, a tartan school dress, nightgown, playsuit, blouse, pedal pushers, bonnet, extra shoes, socks, and curlers to primp her Saran wig. Binnie walks, too, turns her head and closes her eyes. She's made of hard plastic, measures 15 inches tall. Cardboard suitcase with plastic handle is 17⅛x12x5 inches. For ages 6 to 12.
151 T7-B **$19.95**

44.

Winsome Binnie Walker (*Cissy* face): HP; 25in (64cm) head turning walker; red curly hair; original tagged clothes; pink organdy dress; white lace hat; black shoes; white ankle socks; 1954-1955.

> MARKS: "Alexander" (head)
> SEE: *Illustration 45* (Color Section, page 40).
> PRICE: $225-275 15in (38cm)
> $250-300 18in (46cm)
> $325-400 25in (64cm)

Mary Ellen: HP with vinyl arms jointed at elbow; 31in (79cm); jointed at neck, shoulders, elbows, hips, knees; glued-on Saran wig; dressed in red taffeta redingote over dotted white taffeta (used on *Binnie Walker* the same year); white straw hat; exclusive outfit made for Marshall Field & Co.; 1955.

> MARKS: "MME ALEXANDER" (head); "#3122 Mary Ellen" (box)
> SEE: *Illustration 46. Marge Meisinger Collection.*
> PRICE: $425-500

46.

Mary Ellen: additional outfits in the Alexander catalogs.

1954

1. Long party dress of nylon net and lace over taffeta. She has pink satin slippers to match her pink satin sash. There is a circlet of flowers in her hair. She wears white kid gloves.
2. Heavy pile fleece red coat with brass buttons over a taffeta dress. A muff and hat are of leopard plush. She wears suede slippers and carries a hatbox with curlers and comb.
3. Nautical outfit consisting of a tailored dress with a pleated red taffeta skirt, a blue wool middy jacket with brass buttons and white collar and a white French beret with a red pompon. She wears white gloves and suede slippers.

1955

1. Period gown of aqua blue taffeta with tight bodice and bouffant skirt. There is a bonnet and wrist muff made of matching tulle and trimmed with rosebuds. The slippers are pink satin.
2. Bridesmaid's gown of shimmering yellow taffeta which is trimmed with gold braid, appliqued flowers and rhinestones. The hat is a band with tiny flowers and gold mesh veil at each ear. The slippers are pink satin.

PRICE: $50-80 (mint-in-box outfit)

Lissy: HP; 12in (31cm); for general characteristics, see *Hard Plastic Dolls, I*, page 30. *Lissy* is very popular with collectors and is not as easy to find as some of the other Alexander dolls. She came as a bride, bridesmaid or ballerina. A wide selection of separate clothes and accessories were available. There was also a set of *Little Women* dolls (see *Hard Plastic Dolls, I*, page 32). In 1962 *Katie* and *Tommy* were made with a *Lissy* face for the 100th anniversary of F.A.O. Schwarz; in 1962 and 1963 a trousseau set with a doll called *Pamela* was made (see *Glamour Dolls of the 1950s & 1960s*, page 43).

MARKS: None (doll); most clothing marked with Alexander label

47.

48.

SEE: *Illustration 47. Nancy Roeder Collection.*

PRICE: $350-400

Kelly: HP; 12in (31cm); *Lissy* face; unjointed arms and legs; flat feet; (see *Hard Plastic Dolls, I* for comparison of *Lissy* and *Kelly*); pink nylon party dress with ruffles; 1959.

Lissy and *Kelly* were offered in a basic box with underwear or dressed in marked dresses. The 1958 Alexander catalog states that there was a large selection of clothes available. This dress was shown on a hanger with other clothes.

MARKS: None (doll)

SEE: *Illustration 48. Nancy Roeder Collection.*

PRICE: $400-500

Cissy:
Most of the doll manufacturers stopped making all-hard plastic dolls after 1957-1958. The Alexander Doll Company was one of the few that continued making some of them on into the 1960s. Like other companies, they did make some transitional dolls with vinyl heads.

Madame Alexander was a leader in the movement toward a more mature type of doll for children and her hard plastic *Cissy* was one of the first to have a high heel. A detailed explanation of the impact of *Cissy* on the doll world can be found in the *Glamour Dolls of the 1950s & 1960s. Elise*, a few years later, was also an all-hard plastic doll except for her arms. Because the hard plastic era spanned the decade from 1947 to 1957, *Cissy* was included in *Hard Plastic Dolls, I*, and some more pictures are included in this book. However, *Elise* fits the time frame of the book, *Glamour Dolls of the 1950s & 1960s* and her clothes for the most part reflect the fashions of that period. For more detailed information about *Elise* and her clothes, see *Glamour Dolls of the 1950s & 1960s*, pages 33 to 37. An *Elise Renoir* is pictured in *Illustration 51* (Color Section, page 95).

Cissy: HP head, body and legs; vinyl jointed arms; 20in (51cm) to 21in (53cm); high-heel feet; mature body; beautiful red taffeta formal with sweeping skirt; frothy sheer dotted swiss tulle stole that falls to the hem; ring; pearl necklace; circa 1957-1958.
  MARKS: "Alexander" (head)
  SEE: Front cover.
  PRICE: $800 up

Cissy: #2283; silk ball gown with printed camellias; long cape stole of velvet lined to match gown; rhinestone pin at neckline; rhinestone necklace and matching solitaire earrings and ring; gold veil with matching flowers in hair; nylon panties; silk stockings; red high-heeled sandals; full hoop skirt; 1958.
  MARKS: "Alexander" (head)
  SEE: *Illustration 49. Glenn Mandeville Collection.*
  PRICE: $700-800 up

Renoir Cissy: HP; 20in (51cm); long yellow satin dress with matching jacket; black sequin trim and handbag; net petticoat; black sandals; hat made of roses, violets and field flowers with black veil; "diamond" ring; 1961.
  SEE: *Illustration 50. Marianne Gardner Collection.*
  PRICE: $700-800 up

49.

50.

Elise Renoir: HP head and body with vinyl arms; 16½in (42cm); sleep eyes; high-heeled feet; mauve taffeta dress trimmed with lace; silk braid with reticule to match; cameo brooch; solitaire engagement ring; earrings; white straw hat trimmed with field flowers and pink veil; patented wig that can be washed and curled; 1963.

    MARKS: "MME//Alexander" (back); "Alexander" (head)

    SEE: *Illustration 51* (Color Section, page 95).

    PRICE: $550-600

Cissette:

By 1957 most of the doll companies had almost totally ceased using the "injection mold" process for making hard plastic dolls. Most of the children and their mothers preferred the softer vinyl dolls with rooted hair and since the hard plastic doll was more expensive, the era of hard plastic dolls was almost over.

The Alexander Doll Company was an exception. They continued to make the *Cissette* and Alexander-Kin dolls of hard plastic. In 1957 they introduced *Cissette* which is still one of their most popular dolls. She had a slim, mature figure with lovely arms and legs and high-heeled feet. She competed with the small fashion dolls that led to the *Barbie*® fashion era.

Madame Alexander was an acknowledged expert in the entire fashion industry and *Cissette* wore the wonderful clothes of the glamorous years from 1957 to 1963. Her wardrobe was spectacular!

Cissette's wardrobe included street wear, sports outfits, formal gowns and historical period costumes. In 1961 an elegant doll with a special hairdo named *Margo* was part of the line. In 1962 *Cissette* was dressed as Jacqueline Kennedy. She had an unusual dark wig with a side part, a forehead curl and a row of soft curls at the collar line. From 1968 to 1973 a series of Portrette dolls with dazzling costumes was made. The Alexander Doll Company still uses hard plastic for the dolls for their new *Cissette* series.

Today this wonderful doll has been revived to the delight of collectors, and she is as beautiful and glamorous as ever.

Barbie® is a registered trademark of Mattel, Inc.

Cissette: HP; 10½in (27cm); adult body; high heeled; jointed at knees; dressed in light blue toreador pants; fancy nylon blouse; large pink nylon sash; pink rose at neckline; "diamond" earrings; pearl necklace.

    MARKS: "MME Alexander" (back)

    SEE: *Illustration 52* (Color Section, page 39).

    PRICE: $275-300

53.

Cissette Portrette: 10½in (27cm); adult body; high heeled; jointed at knees.
Gold Rush (left): orange taffeta dress with black lace; black picture hat; 1963.
Gibson Girl (right): dark purple skirt; white and lavender striped blouse; purple hat with lavender feathers; 1963.
    MARKS: "Mme Alexander" (back)
    SEE: *Illustration 53. Louise Schnell Collection.*
    PRICE: $1400 (*Gold Rush*) $1200 (*Gibson Girl*)

Cissette Portrette: HP; 10½in (27cm); high heeled; jointed at knees.
Renoir (left): long dark blue dress trimmed with lace; red picture hat; 1968.
Scarlett (middle): dark green taffeta dress with black trim; green picture hat with white feather; 1968.
Agatha (right): red dress with lace trim; hat missing; 1968.
    MARKS: "Mme Alexander" (back)
    SEE: *Illustration 54. Louise Schnell Collection.*
    PRICE: $500-600 (*Renoir*) $500-550 (*Scarlett*) $575-595 (*Agatha*)

54.

Cissette Portrette: HP; 10½in (27cm); adult body; high heeled; jointed at knees.
Godey (left): pink taffeta dress with two ruffles at hemline; pink picture hat; 1968.
Southern Belle (middle): white dress with pleated ruffle at bottom of skirt; trimmed with lace with green ribbon running through it; large net picture hat trimmed with red roses; 1968.
Melinda (right): blue taffeta dress with ruffle at hemline; white lace collar; bonnet-type hat with blue net trim with ties at neck; 1968.
    MARKS: "Mme Alexander" (back)
    SEE: *Illustration 55 (Color Section, page 39). Louise Schnell Collection.*
    PRICE: $500-575 (*Godey*) $500-575 (*Southern Belle*) $475-550 (*Melinda*)

56.

Jenny Lind: HP; 11in (28cm); high-heeled feet; jointed at knees; Portrette 1969; pink satin dress with pink satin over skirt; trimmed in lace; light and dark pink rosebud bouquet; blonde hair has center part and pulled to each side and fastened with rosebuds.
    SEE: *Illustration 56. Vivien Brady-Ashley Collection.*
    PRICE: $700-750+

Alexander-kins

The small 7½in (19cm) to 8in (20cm) dolls were first sold in 1953 and are still being sold today. Mothers and grandmothers started collections for their children because they were inexpensive and beautiful. The international dolls have helped children learn the countries of the world for the last 35 years. Many adult collectors consider that these dolls are the base of their collections. The newest tiny Alexanders are eagerly anticipated each year at the American International Toy Fair. Orders are quickly placed in local stores and new dolls join the beloved older ones.

Along with the international dolls, other small *Wendy Ann/Wendy/Wendi-kins/ Alexander-kins*, as they have been called, were in the Alexander catalogs each year. Over the years there has been an interest in these dolls by a group of collectors who have become specialists. The entire world of the regular *Wendy-kins, Alexander-kins* is different from the other world of Alexander doll collecting. Unexpectedly, these dolls have appreciated in price to a greater degree than most of the other Alexander dolls; a few sometimes command prices of over $1000. The list of dolls below is printed with the hope that collectors will be able to identify those rare dolls that seem to be selling at the highest prices.

1953
1. *Agatha*
2. *Blue Danube*
3. *Civil War*
4. *Edwardian*
5. *Goya*
6. *Guardian Angel*
7. *Little Godey*
8. *Madeline*
9. *Little Southern Girl*
10. *Little Victoria*
11. *Peter Pan*
12. *Quiz-kin*
13. *Quiz-kin Bride*
14. *Quiz-kin Ballerina*
15. *Victoria*

1954
1. *Bible Characters*
2. *Agatha*
3. *Apple Annie*
4. *Blue Danube*
5. *Civil War*
6. *Elaine*
7. *Guardian Angel*
8. *Little Godey*
9. *Little Victoria*
10. *Mary Louise*
11. *Queen*
12. *Southern Belle*
13. *Victoria*
14. *Wendy Angel*

1955
1. *Garden Party*
   (long gown; both straight leg
   non-walker and walker)

2. *Baby Angel*
3. *Baby Clown*
4. *The Best Man*
5. *Bridesmaid*
6. *Curly-Locks*
7. *Davy Crockett Boy and Girl*
8. *Drum Majorette*
9. *Dude Ranch*
10. *Highland Fling*
11. *Juliet*
12. *Majorette*
13. *Melanie*
14. *Lady in Waiting*
15. *Little Minister*
16. *Mambo*
17. *Red Riding Hood*
18. *Rodeo*
19. *Romeo*
20. *Southern Belle*
21. *Waltzing*

1956
1. *Ballerina*
2. *Bridesmaid*
3. *Cousin Karen*
4. *Flower girl*
5. *Little Melanie*
6. *Melanie*
7. *Nurse*
8. *Parlour Maid*
9. *Pierrot Clown*
10. *Southern Belle*
11. *Story Princess*

1957
1. *Aunt Agatha*

31

2. *Aunt Pitty Pat*
3. *Bride*
4. *Bridesmaid*
5. *Cousin Grace*
6. *First Communion*
7. *Groom*
8. *Governess Nana*
9. *Graduation Party*
10. *Little Minister*
11. *Prince Charles*
12. *Princess Ann*

1958
1. *Bridesmaid*
2. *Edith the Lonely Doll*

1960
1. *Little Lady with Box of Cosmetics*

1961
1. *Amanda of Americana Group*
2. *Charity of Americana Group*
3. *Faith of Americana Group*
4. *Lucy of Americana Group*
5. *Maggie Mixup*
6. *Maggie Mixup Angel*
7. *Maggie Mixup with Watering Can*
8. *Maggie Mixup in Skating Costume*
9. *Maggie Mixup in Riding Habit*

1963
1. *Southern Belle*

1965
1. *1965-1972 Sewing Kit and Doll*

1968
1. *Easter Doll*

PRICES: Since there is a limited number of people willing to pay high prices for these dolls, local prices may be considerably less than national prices. To get the top prices, the seller may have to advertise nationally or even internationally.

57.

Davy Crockett Boy and Girl: HP; 8in (20cm); straight leg walker; boy has red caracul wig; girl has red "flip style" wig; both have mock suede clothes with fringe; belts have metal buckles; plush "coonskin" caps; 1955.

    SEE: *Illustration 57. Margaret Mandel Collection.*

    PRICE: $800-1000+ each

Continued on page 41.

Alexander *Champs-Elysees* (see page 20). *Vivien Brady-Ashley Collection.*

Alexander *Victorian Bride* (see page 21). *Sandra Crane Collection.*

Alexander *Judy* (see page 21). *Diane Huffman Collection.*

Alexander *Pink Champagne* (see page 21). *Vivien Brady-Ashley Collection.*

Alexander *Deborah* (see page 21). *Sandra Crane Collection.*

Alexander *Kathryn Grayson* (see page 21). *Sandra Crane Collection*

Alexander *Cissette Portrettes* (left to right): *Godey Lady, Southern Belle, Melinda* (see page 30). *Louise Schnell Collection.*

Alexander *Cissette* in toreador pants (see page 29).

Alexander *Binnie Walker* (see page 26).

Alexander *Cinderella* (see page 19).

Continued from page 32.

Infant of Prague: HP; 8in (20cm); bent knee walker; unusual construction of hand; right hand molded so palm is in down position with 3rd finger curled under; left palm of hand faces upward; ornate jeweled crown and clothes; circa 1956.
  SEE: *Illustration 58. Vivien Brady-Ashley Collection.*
  PRICE: Not enough sample prices.

Angel: HP; 8in (20cm); *Maggie Mixup* face; bent knee walker; pink robe with gold trim; wings covered with gold design; circa 1960-1961.
  MARKS: "Alex" (back)
  SEE: *Illustration 59. Nancy Roeder Collection.*
  PRICE: $1200-1500 up

58.   59.

Bride and Groom: HP; 8in (20cm); bent knee walker; circa 1957.
  MARKS: "Alex" (back)
  SEE: *Illustration 60. Nancy Roeder Collection.*
  PRICE: $900-1000 pair

60.

61.

Little Women: HP; 8in (20cm); bent knee walker.

Madame Alexander loved to design dolls from fiction and the characters from *Little Women* were among her favorites. Most of the hard plastic dolls in various sizes were used for these famous dolls. The small dolls known as Alexander-kins have been used for these character dolls for many years and are still favorites with children and collectors.

> SEE: *Illustration 61. Toys and Novelties,* March 1964.
> PRICE: $650-725 set

62.

Little Genius: HP head and "Magic Skin" arms and legs; cloth body; 19in (46cm); eye shadow above eyes; hair in original set; all original yellow nylon dress with matching hat; matching yellow taffeta panties; dress trimmed with flowers; also came in 16in (41cm) and 23in (58cm); circa 1949.

> MARKS: "Little Genius//Alexander N.Y. U.S.A.//All Rights Reserved" (dress) "Alexander" (head)
> SEE: *Illustration 62. Mary Ann Bauman Collection.*
> PRICE: $275-325

Quiz-kin: HP; 7½in (19cm); straight leg non-walker; named after the television "Quiz Kids;" two buttons in back to make head move; all original pink organdy dress; 1953.

> SEE: *Illustration 63. Dorothy Hesner Collection.*
> PRICE: $400-550

63.

American Character Doll Co.

American Character Doll Co. was a leader in the manufacturing of dolls in the hard plastic era. In 1952 they published a catalog of the dolls made that year. On the first page they said, "For 33 years the American Character Doll Co. has manufactured dolls of the finest quality and craftsmanship, catering to children of all age groups.

"Our dolls have always appealed to parents because of their durability, and to children because of their beauty and play value.

"Some of our famous dolls that have become American 'Buy-words' are *TOODLES*, the first rubber doll; *SWEET SUE*, the first dolls with Saran wigs that could be washed, combed and curled; *TINY TEARS*, the only doll ever made that cries with real, wet tears."

SEE: *Illustrations 64* through *77*; These are the hard plastic dolls from this catalog.

Tiny Tears Characteristics: there are several different *Tiny Tears* dolls.
1. HP head; 18½in (47cm); rubber body which squeaks when pressed; very heavy doll (over four pounds); mouth with hole in it for bottle; sleep eyes with lashes; hole in nostrils close to eyes for tears; dimples above toes on feet and below fingers on hands; molded hair; circa 1950.
2. HP head; 15in (38cm); vinyl body; plastic has waxy look; mouth with hole for bottle; sleep eyes with lashes; holes in nostrils close to eyes for tears; dimples above toes on feet and below fingers on hands; individual fingers; rooted hair inset in skull cap; clothes not original; circa 1952 to 1955.
3. HP head; 12in (31cm); all-rubber body; mouth with hole for bottle; sleep eyes with lashes; holes in nostrils close to eyes for tears; individual fingers with dimples below fingers on hands and dimples above toes on feet; rubber body squeaks when pressed; head measures 11in (28cm) in circumference; molded hair; circa 1950.
4. HP head; 11in (28cm); vinyl arms, legs and body; plastic has waxy look; mouth with hole for bottle; sleep eyes with lashes; hole in nostrils close to eyes for tears; dimples above toes on feet and below fingers on hands; body squeaks when pressed; head 10in (25cm) in circumference; individual fingers; molded hair; circa 1952-1955.

Each of these types of dolls may come in different sizes. For pictures of these dolls see *Hard Plastic Dolls, I*, pages 48 to 50.

Sweet Sue Characteristics:
1. Rather light skin color but there is some blush in the checks.
2. The hair is coarse, rough and difficult to curl but it is pretty and washable.
3. The walkers have a spring in the arm joint which is distinctive to these dolls.
4. Many dresses are full-skirted with an attempt to imitate the hoop skirt, especially in formal wear. The sleeves are often puffed below the elbow.
5. Shoes often have a snap closing.
6. Most wigs are blonde or reddish blonde.
7. Mouth is slightly off center.
8. Closed mouth.
9. Sleep eyes with lashes.

Sweet Sue Marks:
1. "A.C."
2. "Amer. Char."
3. Many of the dolls were unmarked.
   PRICE: $135-150   14in (36cm)
      $170-200   18in (46cm) - 20in (51cm)
      $235-250   24in (61cm)
      $275-350   30in (76cm)

Sweet Sue School Girl: HP; 14½in (37cm); dainty print dress of white embossed cotton with matching panties; neckline and circular skirt edged with pleated scalloped trim; two roses nestled at neckline; Saran hair gathered with two bows; doll on right is pictured in 1952 company catalog; doll on left wears the same dress.
   MARKS: None
   SEE: *Illustration 64. Sharlene Doyle Collection* (doll on left).
   PRICE: $135-150

Sweet Sue Birthday Party (left): light blue taffeta party dress with matching panties; French piping on neckline, waist and flounce; Saran hair with a rose and pink velvet bow.

Sweet Alice (right): blue satin-finished broadcloth dress; sheer white cross-bar lace-trimmed organdy pinafore; matching blue panties; long blonde Saran hair with black velvet bow; black patent leather pumps.
   SEE: *Illustration 65.*

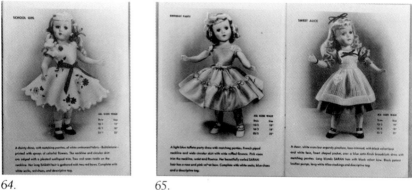

64.   65.

Sweet Alice: HP; 16½in (38cm); turning head walker; arm hooked to heavy springs; closed mouth; sleep eyes; long blonde Saran wig; mouth off center; lashes painted under eyes; sheer white cross-bar organdy pinafore, lace trimmed; black velvet bow; blue satin-finish broadcloth dress with matching panties; black patent leather pumps; long white "Alice" stockings; in 1952 catalog. (For general American *Sweet Sue* characteristics, see page 43.)
   MARKS: "Made in U.S.A." (back)
   SEE: *Illustration 66* (Color Section, page 162).
   PRICE: $150-160

Sweet Sue Bride (left): heavy white satin gown with deep ruffle around skirt; Queen Elizabeth neckline with lace and satin ribbons; nylon tulle veil with lace and lillies of the valley trim; wired hoop slip and matching panties.

Mardi Gras (right): satin formal gown; circular skirt; deep cowl off-the-shoulder neckline; large pouf sash of contrasting color; ruffled hoop slip; matching panties; long Saran glamour bob pinned back with a rose; silver slippers.

SEE: *Illustration 67.* American Character 1952 catalog.

PRICE: $135-160   15in (38cm)
$170-200   18in (46cm)
$225-250   23in (58cm)

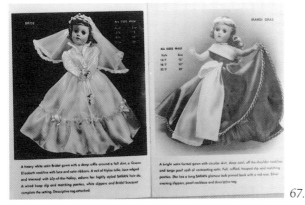

67.

Sweet Sue Co-Ed (left): red and green tartan taffeta with full skirt; important braid trim; "Gibson Girl" organdy sleeves; deep neckline with revers trimmed with lace; long wavy Saran hair.

Sunday Best (right): red taffeta brocade button-down dress; matching panties; deep white collar and cuffs trimmed with Val lace; straw hat over curled Saran hair; white parasol.

SEE: *Illustration 68.* American Character 1952 catalog.

68.

45

Sweet Sue Cotillion: a dream dress of satin lace; full skirt over taffeta slip; front is shirred nylon tulle ruffles; pink and blue rosebuds scattered over the tulle; form-fitting satin bodice; lace-edged flaired shoulder ruffles; ruffled hooped slip; matching panties; pearl necklace; satin slippers; hair is a Saran ponytail; matching chignon in carrying case.

SEE: *Illustration 69.* American Character 1952 catalog.

PRICE: $225-300

Tiny Tears: catalog says, "The only doll that cries real tears. Feed her she wets; place a pacifier in her mouth, squeeze her gently, and she weeps big, wet tears. You can hear her cry lustily. *Tiny Tears* drinks her bottle, wets her diaper, blows big soap bubbles, sleeps and can be bathed. She is made of molded rubber — fully jointed — and has a plastic head, sleeping eyes and lashes."

MARKS: "American Character" (head); some dolls have "Pat. No. 2.675.644" (head)

SEE: *Illustration 69.* American Character 1952 catalog.

PRICE: $50-55   11in (28cm)
$50-55   12in (31cm)
$50-55   15in (38cm)
$80-85   18½in (47cm)

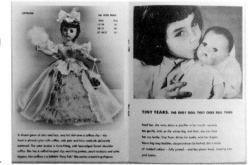

69.

American Character Doll Company advertised widely on television. In connection with the "The Pinky Lee Show," they published a small cartoon and advertising doll book which cost 15 cents. Along with cartoon adventures of *Tiny Tears*, *Sweet Sue* and *Toodles*, pictures of the actual dolls in the 1955 line were shown in beautiful color. The cover is shown in *Illustration 70. Illustration 71* shows two adventures of *Sweet Sue*. 1. *Sweet Sue* stars on Pinky's T.V. show. 2. Life size *Sweet Sue* fools Pinky Lee.

SEE: *Illustration 70.*
Illustration 71.   70.

71.

Life Size *Sweet Sue:* HP body and legs; vinyl arms; jointed at neck, shoulders, elbows, hips, knees; as big as a three-year-old-child; walks, sits, stands, kneels; rooted hair in vinyl head.

    SEE: *Illustration 72* pictured in *Adventures of Pinky Lee, Tiny Tears,* and *Sweet Sue* published by American Character Doll Company, 1955.

    PRICE: $275-300

72.

Sweet Sue wardrobe from 1955 catalog "Adventures of *Pinky Lee, Tiny Tears,* and *Sweet Sue"*; published by American Character Doll Company. From left to right top row: *Springtime, Sweet Sue Coat, Sunday Best, Junior Prom.* From left to right middle row: *Birthday Party, Co-ed, Cotillion, Bride.* From left to right bottom row: *Schoolgirl, Teatime, Life Size Sweet Sue.*

    SEE: *Illustration 73.* (Color Section, page 96).

Tiny Tears: HP head; jointed rubber body; 13in (33cm); both doll and layette were featured on the television program "Ding Dong School;" doll cries real tears if she is fed water from her bottle. The pacifier is placed in her mouth and then she is gently squeezed; doll also wets, blows bubbles, sleeps; doll is washable; layette includes embossed cotton dress, panties, bonnet, knit booties, sleeping garment, extra diaper, package of Kleenex tissues, bottle, sponge, soap, bubble pipe, washcloth, pacifier, instruction booklet; 1954.

    MARKS: "American Character" (head); some dolls have "Pat. No. 2.675.644" (head)

    SEE: *Illustration 74.* Marshall Field & Co. 1954 Christmas catalog. *Barbara Andresen Collection.*

    PRICE: $55-60

Tiny Tears and her layette featured on Ding Dong School. Just feed her water from her bottle, place pacifier in her mouth, squeeze her gently, she cries real tears. She wets, blows bubbles, sleeps, can be bathed. Has movable, jointed rubber body and hard plastic head. Layette includes: embossed cotton dress, panties, bonnet, knit bootees, sleeping garment, extra diaper, package of Kleenex tissues, bottle, sponge, soap, bubble pipe, washcloth, pacifier and instruction booklet. 13 inches tall. For girls ages 4 to 10.
151 T2-64 ....$7.95

74.

Toodles "Potty Baby": HP head and molded rubber body; 13in (33cm) and 16in (41cm); advertisement first appeared in *Life Magazine*; the advertisement said "'Toodles the Potty Baby' makes a game out of teaching little girls the rules of baby care." The doll came with a layette. Other dolls advertised in 1949 included *Baby Sue*, *Sweet Sue* and *Little Sis* (a rubber doll).

SEE: *Illustration 75. Playthings*, October 1949.

PRICE: $50-70

75.

Annie Oakley: HP; 18in (46cm); fully jointed; unusual face; red and white cowgirl outfit; blonde hair; sleep eyes with unusual feathered eyebrows; eyelashes below the eyes and five lines to the side of the eye; arm hook (see Identification Guide, *Hard Plastic Dolls, I*, page 266P); 1955.

MARKS: Small "P" (arm hook).

SEE: *Illustration 76* (doll). *Diane Loney Collection.*

Illustration 77. American Character Doll Co. catalog, 1955.

PRICE: $170-200 (complete)

76.

77.

Betsy McCall: HP; 8in (20cm); beautiful bisque-like finish; rooted brown hair in a plastic skull cap covering or wig; blue sleep eyes with molded lashes; closed mouth; knee joints; 2nd and 3rd fingers molded together. *Betsy* has clothes which could be purchased, and *McCalls* magazine featured *Betsy* and her wardrobe each month in paper doll form; white and red gingham dress with white bias trim at neckline; white apron; all original; circa 1958. *Betsy McCall's* hair was either a wig or a plastic skull cap with inset hair.

MARKS: "McCall Corporation" (on back in circle)
SEE: *Illustration 78.*
PRICE: $100-120

78.

Arranbee Doll Company, Inc.

The Arranbee Company was a maker of fine dolls in the early 1950s, and the following pictures show the lovely dolls and their clothes.

It is interesting that in 1951 they were ahead of their time and were experimenting with vinyl dolls and parts. The *Nancy* doll was advertised as having a vinyl head, arms and legs. It was one of the few dolls with a vinyl head that had a wig. It was also one of the few hard plastic dolls made in the United States with a "Mama" voice box. (See *Illustration 79.*) A baby made that year also had a vinyl head. Most of the other dolls in their line were all-hard plastic.

The company was interested in clothes and fashion. The little girl dolls were dressed in the type of dresses fashionable for the little girls who owned them. They also made formal designer-type doll clothes for the older girls.

The 11in (28cm) *Littlest Angel* dolls were among their best sellers. They were *Ginny*-type dolls that were larger and easier to manipulate than the small 8in (20cm) walking dolls. Today they are beloved by many collectors because of their cute "chubby" bodies and beautiful clothes.

In 1957, just before Arranbee was sold, they advertised an all-vinyl doll with 12 outfits. The book *Glamour Dolls of the 1950s & 1960s*, shows pictures of some of the vinyl dolls and company catalogs made when Arranbee became a division of Vogue.

Nanette: HP; 15in (38cm), 18in (46cm) and 23in (58cm); non-walking; sleep eyes; Dynel or Saran wig; came with comb, curlers and two-color instruction sheet; 1950.

1. (Upper right) *Party Formal*: full length sheer over ruffled satin hooped slip; picture hat.
2. (Center) *Roller Skater*: wide belted plaid jumper; peasant blouse; matching hair ribbon; roller skates.
3. (Lower left) *Tea Party*; short taffeta print party dress with ribbons and bows; carrying a little handbag.

  SEE: *Illustration 79. Playthings*, October 1950.

  PRICE: $140-165   15in (36cm)
    depending on outfit
    $180-220   18in (46cm)
    depending on outfit
    $225-300   23in (58cm)
    depending on outfit

79.

Ginny® is a registered trademark of Vogue Dolls, Inc.

Nanette Cowgirl: HP; 14in (36cm); red felt skirt; black and white plaid top; black felt dress with silver trim; yellow tie; red felt cowboy hat; red felt boots with white trim; circa 1950-1956.

 MARKS: "R&B" (head)
 SEE: *Illustration 80. Marianne Gardner Collection.*
 PRICE: $150-180 (complete)

Nanette with Tiara: HP; 18in (46cm); head-turning walker; jointed at neck, arms and hips; beautiful plastic with excellent skin tone; red wig; sleep eyes with lashes under eyes; 2nd and 3rd fingers molded together; pink embroidered net formal dress over pink taffeta slip; white slip with hoop; pearl straps; pink flowers at waist; silver tiara on head; early 1950s.

 MARKS: "R&B" (head)
 SEE: *Illustration 81.*
 PRICE: $160-180

Nancy Lee: HP; 14in (36cm); deep rose velvet ball gown trimmed with feathers; pair of white half gloves; white cotton purse trimmed with gold braid; white anklets; gold shoes; tosca wig; all original; circa early 1950s.

 MARKS: "R&B" (head)
 SEE: *Illustration 82* (Color Section, page 96). *Lois Janner Collection.*
 PRICE: $150-180

80.

81.

51

Nancy Lee Skater: HP; 20in (51cm) without skates; blonde mohair wig; sleep eyes; all original red and white skating outfit; white skates; circa early 1950s.

MARKS: "R&B" (head); "Nancy Lee 14106//R & B Quality Doll" (box)

SEE: *Illustration 83. Vivian Brady-Ashley Collection.*

PRICE: $250-300

83.

Nancy: HP; 14in (36cm); lovely skin tone with red on cheeks, hands and knees; pink skating outfit with various colors on trim around the skirt; all original including ice skates; circa early 1950s.

MARKS: "Nancy" (tag)

SEE: *Illustration 84. Sandy Strater Collection.*

PRICE: $150-180

Nancy: HP body with vinyl arms, legs and head; 24in (61cm); walker; washable Dynel hair; says "Mama;" clothes patterned after children's clothes. This is a very unusual early Arranbee doll. During this period manufacturers were experimenting with the various types of plastic and vinyl. It is unusual to find a vinyl-headed doll with a wig. Other dolls advertised were *Angel Face* which also had a vinyl head, arms and legs; all-HP *Nannette; Dream Baby* with a soft vinyl head.

SEE: *Illustration 85. Playthings,* July 1951.

84.

85.

Life Size *Nanette:* plastic body with soft vinyl head; 30in (76cm) head turning walker; sleep eyes; washable rooted Saran hair that can be combed and curled; came with four costumes; 1955.

SEE: *Illustration 86.* 1955 Arranbee catalog. *Kathryn Davis Collection.*

PRICE: $275-350

86.

***Nanette* Brochure:** HP with vinyl head; 15in (38cm), 18in (46cm) and 25in (64cm); head turning walker; jointed at neck, shoulders, hips and knees; sleep eyes; closed mouth; rooted Saran hair; individual fingers; guaranteed not to crack, peel or chip; 1955.

MARKS: "17VW" (head)

SEE: *Illustration 87.* 1955 Arranbee catalog. *Kathryn Davis Collection.*
Illustration 88. 1955 Arranbee catalog. *Kathryn Davis Collection.*

87.

88.

Nanette Ballerina: HP with vinyl head; 18in (46cm); head turning walker; real lashes; sleep eyes; painted lashes under eyes; closed mouth; auburn rooted hair; individual fingers; jointed at neck, shoulders, hips and knees; peach satin bodice; beige net tutu with printed stars and circles; pink flowers at neckline; flat feet with pink ballet slippers; 1955. These dolls also came in a 15in (38cm) size. On her tag Arranbee advertised *Littlest Angel, Sweet Pea, Angel Face, Angel Skin* and *Dream Baby.*

  MARKS: "17VW" (back of head); "R&B Nanette//kneels//walks//sits//stands//turns her head//My Saran Hair is Rooted just like real Growing hair" (tag)
  SEE: *Illustration 89.*
  PRICE: $100-125

Nanette Beauty Shop Doll: HP; 15in (38cm); 18in (46cm) and 23in (58cm); head turning walker; complete with curlers and easy instructions for doing hair. The Arranbee doll at the bottom of the page in the middle is an all-vinyl *Nancy Lee* doll with 12 outfits.
  SEE: *Illustration 90. Playthings*, August 1957.

89.   90.

Littlest Angel All-HP Characteristics: 10½in (27cm) - 11in (28cm); open-closed mouth with slightly molded tongue; sleep eyes with molded eyelashes; painted eyelashes below the eye; hip pin walker (see Identification Guide, *Hard Plastic Dolls, I*, page 291D); 1954 dolls have straight legs; later dolls have jointed knees; individual fingers with 3rd and 4th fingers curving slightly inward; dimples above fingers and toes; arm hooks (see Identification Guide, pages 236). It is possible for these dolls to have no mark. However, the best clue to identification is the hip pin walker.
  MARKS: Most have "R&B" (head); the "R&B" is not always distinct and can wear off.

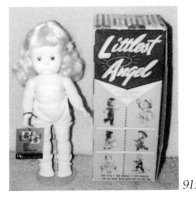
91.

Littlest Angel: HP; 11in (28cm); jointed at neck, shoulders, hips and knees; head turning walker; basic doll came with panties, shoes, socks, tag and box which showed some of the outfits; 1955. Boxed outfits were usually purchased separately, SEE: *Illustration 91. Sally Herbst Collection.*
PRICE: $55-75

Littlest Angel **Brochure 1954: "The Busiest Girl We Know"**

1. *Two Piece Sleeper:* yellow and blue knitted sleeper; little lamb embroidered on top.
2. *Sunsuit and Hat:* red and white sunsuit which can be used as a swimsuit. (See *Illustration 100.*)
3. *Sunsuit and Straw Hat:* blue sunsuit trimmed with lace; large straw hat.
4. *Three-Piece Pajama Set:* Two-piece pajamas with elegant matching robe and slippers.
5. *Afternoon Dress:* red and white peppermint dress; lace trimming; matching panties.
6. *Tennis Ensemble:* white shorts; blue and white halter and shirt; tennis cap; tennis racket.
7. *Organdy Birthday Dress:* dress with pink rosebuds; ruffles.
8. *School Dress:* lace-trimmed polka dot swiss organdy dress; magic slate and pencil.
9. *Overalls and Hat:* red and white checkered overalls and matching bonnet.
10. *Garden Party Dress:* pink dress with embroidery; rosebuds at waist; natural color straw bonnet.
11. *Beach Apparel:* bathing suit; salmon-colored robe and hood; special beach bag; slippers.
12. *Skating Costume:* black felt with silver trim; black hat; silver skates.
13. *Nurse's Uniform:* traditional nylon nurse's uniform; blue cape with red lining.
14. *Picnic Outfit:* pedal pushers; frilly peasant blouse; gold slippers; glasses.
15. *Bridal Gown:* gown embroidered with tiny flowers; illusion net veil; bridal bouquet.
16. *Formal Gown:* ruffled long dress; gold slippers.
17. *Roller Skating Set:* dungarees with red polka dot cuffs; matching handkerchief; halter; bonnet.
18. *Coat, Hat, Dress:* stylish hat and coat; lace trim; Christmas dress under coat.
19. *Fisherman's Outfit:* denim pants; shirt with fish on it; green straw hat; black boots; two fish and other fishing equipment in bag.
20. *Drum Majorette Costume:* fancy skirt; satin top with shiny buttons; high-stepping boots; peaked hat with plume.
21. *Ballerina Costume:* pink tulle; pink satin ballet slippers; rosebuds in hair. (See *Illustration 104.*)
22. *Two-Gun Tess:* brown leatherette riding skirt; two-pint hat; riding boots; twin pistols. (See *Illustration 103.*)
23. *Ski Outfit:* blue and white outfit with white ribbing; tassel cap; skis and poles. (See *Illustration 98.*)
24. *TV Lounging Clothes:* blue and silver oriental jacket; lounging slippers; glasses.

Littlest Angel Brochure 1955: all dolls have jointed knees.
SEE: *Illustration 92. Brochure from Kathryn Davis Collection.*

92.

Littlest Angel Brochure 1955:
SEE: *Illustration 93. Brochure from Kathryn Davis Collection.*

93.

Littlest Angel Brochure 1955:
SEE: *Illustration 94. Brochure from Kathryn Davis Collection.*

94.

Littlest Angel Brochure 1955:
    SEE: *Illustration 95. Brochure from Kathryn Davis Collection.*

95.

Littlest Angel Brochure 1955:
    SEE: *Illustration 96. Brochure from Kathryn Davis Collection.*

96.

Littlest Angel Brochure 1955:
    SEE: *Illustration 97. Brochure from Kathryn Davis Collection.*

97.

Littlest Angel Brochure 1955: Not Photographed.
1. *Garment Bag:* plaid garment bag with hanger; #102.
2. *Travel Set:* plaid car bag with zipper: matching tote bag: #103.
3. *Travel Trunk:* metal trunk with drawer; #104.
4. *Gretel Metal Trunk:* trunk with three outfits and doll; sunglasses; extra shoes, socks, hangers; #151.
5. *Riding Habit Metal Trunk:* weekend package with three costumes and doll; hangers; glasses; extra shoes and socks; doll dressed in jodhpurs; #152.

Littlest Angel Brochure 1957 all dolls have jointed knees; buyer had choice of vinyl head with rooted hair (V1010) or hard head with foundation wig (H1010). This catalog had fewer descriptions than the previous two catalogs.

1. *Standard Doll in Box:* dressed only in panties, shoes, socks; #V1010 and #H1010. The doll with the hard head cost $2.59 and the doll with the vinyl head cost $2.98.
2. *R & B Surprise Doll All Packed to Go Bye Bye in Her 4 Color Gift Box: Surprise Doll Book.*
   A. *English Outfit:* #SD-1.
   B. *Chinese Outfit:* #SD-2; (see *Illustration 106*).
   C. *French Outfit:* #SD-3.
   D. *Russian Outfit:* #SD-4.
   E. *Italian Outfit:* #SD-5.
   F. *Dutch Outfit:* #SD-6.
   G. *Dressed Doll and Wonder Book:* #SD-10.
3. *Denim Smock:* #503.
4. *Checked Overalls:* #504.
5. *Ice Skater:* red velvet skating outfit with white trim and pompon; silver skates; matching hat with pompon; #509; (see *Illustration 98*).
6. *Artist's Outfit:* #512.
7. *Gretel Outfit:* #514.
8. *Red Riding Hood:* #516.
9. *Alice in Wonderland:* #517.
10. *Golf Outfit:* #519.
11. *Embroidered Nylon Dress:* #618.
12. *Square Dancer:* #620.
13. *Leather Jacket Set:* #623.
14. *Ballerina Outfit:* #613.
15. *Dress and Reversible Coat:* #612.
16. *Appliqued Nylon Dress:* #61.
17. *Formal Outfit:* #603.
18. *Formal Outfit:* #604.
19. *TV Outfit:* #609.
20. *Nylon Dress and Hat Outfit:* #611.
21. *Ski Outfit:* #616; (see *Illustration 98*).
22. *Cowgirl Outfit:* #607; (see *Illustration 103*).
23. *Riding Habit:* #617; (see Color Section, page 168).
24. *Formal Dress and Hat:* #707.
25. *Bridal Outfit:* #706; (see *Illustration 105*).
26. *Velvet Coat & Formal Dress:* #804.
27. *Borgana Fur Coat:* #709.
28. *Formal Dress with Fur Stole:* #803.
29. *Coat, Hat & Dress Set:* #705.
30. *Aqua Organdy Dress:* #312.
31. *Two-Piece Sleeper:* #301.
32. *Polka Dot Dress:* #310.
33. *Sunsuit and Parasol:* #308; dark suit with fancy trim.
34. *Lantern Print Dress:* #309.
35. *Red Plaid Dress:* #417.
36. *Three-Piece Pajama Set:* #412.
37. *Rain Outfit:* #413.
38. *Organdy Dress and Hat Set:* #414.
39. *Brown Strip Dress:* #416.
40. *Afternoon Dress:* #402; candy stripe and white dress.
41. *Tennis Outfit:* #404.
42. *Party Dress:* #406.
43. *Bermuda Shorts:* #407.
44. *Tic Tac Toe Print Dress:* #528.
45. *Cardigan and Hat:* #523.
46. *School Dress and Hat Set:* striped with print pinafore; #526.
47. *Taffeta Party Dress:* #529.
48. *Nurse's Outfit:* #510.
49. *Pleated Skirt and Blouse:* #527.

Littlest Angel Skier: HP; 11in (28cm); blue gabardine ski outfit with white knit and red braid trim; blue ski hat with white knit trim and pompon; wooden skis attached to black shoes; wood ski poles; outfit listed in 1954. It was listed as #065 in 1955 and #616 in 1957. This particular outfit was purchased mint-in-box which was the way most of the clothes were purchased at the time.

    MARKS: "R&B" (head and body)
    SEE: *Illustration 98.*
    PRICE: $55-75

Littlest Angel Skater: HP with vinyl head; 11in (28cm); red velvet skating costume with white trim; silver ice skates; all original; listed #509 in 1957 catalog. Other skating costumes include a black felt one with silver trim and black hat in 1954 and #054 a white knitted skating suit in 1955.

    MARKS: "R&B Doll Company" (body only)
    SEE: *Illustration 98.*
    PRICE: $45-65

Littlest Angel in Jodhpurs (left): HP; 11in (28cm); white jodhpurs and blouse; red vest, jockey cap, boots; circa 1955-1957.

    MARKS: "R&B" (head)
    SEE: *Illustration 99* (Color Section, page 168).
    PRICE: $75-90

Littlest Angel: HP; 11in (28cm); red and white cotton print sunsuit in 1954 catalog; 1955 doll jointed at neck, shoulders, hips and knees; outfit could double for swimsuit.

    MARKS: "R&B" (head)
    SEE: *Illustration 100. Nancy Carlton Collection.*
    PRICE: $55-75

98.

100.

Littlest Angel: HP; 10in (25cm); walking doll; sleep eyes; Saran wig can be combed and curled; wardrobe includes broadcloth dress, panty, party dress, lacy slip, corduroy coat, hat, organdy dress, overalls, blouse, robe, pajamas, sunsuit, slippers, shoes, socks; 1954.
> SEE: *Illustration 101.* 1954 Marshall Field & Co. Christmas catalog. *Barbara Andresen Collection.*
> PRICE: $80-100

Littlest Angel: HP; 10in (25cm); head turning walker; accessories include a mahogany reproduction of early American Tester bed; two-drawer wardrobe with mahogany finish; 1954.
> SEE: *Illustration 102.* 1954 Marshall Field & Co. catalog. *Barbara Andresen Collection.*
> PRICE: $55-75 (doll)

Littlest Angel has a heavenly wardrobe. She wears dress and panty, and the foot high wood trunk holds: broadcloth dress, panty, party dress, lacy slip, corduroy coat, hat, organdy dress, overalls, blouse, robe and pajama set, sun suit, slippers, shoes and socks. She's 10 inches tall, plastic, walks, sits and stands alone, closes her eyes. Saran wig can be combed and curled for your littlest Christmas angels, ages 4 to 10.
151 T2-87 .... **$15.95**

101.

give her a Doll to play with and love

[F] **Colonial bed** sure to bring sweet sugar plum dreams to any doll. Reproduction of early American Tester bed in fine mahogany finish. Dotted-Swiss canopy and spread, tufted mattress and bolster. 13¾x8½x 13 inches, big enough for 8-inch doll. Ages 4 to 10. **151 T2-89**...**$7.95**
[G] **Littlest Angel.** 151 T2-88—10-inch doll in red pajamas........$4
[H] **Two drawer wardrobe** with lots of room for pretend-mothers to store their children's clothes. Fine mahogany finish. Deep sliding drawers. 13½x9x5 inches, will hold wardrobe for dolls up to 11 inches tall. For girls age 4 to 10. **151 T2-90** **$7.95**

11

102.

103.

104.

Littlest Angel Cowgirl: HP; 10½in (27cm); braided blonde wig with flowers in hair; blue eyes; all original cowgirl dress with brown leather-type skirt, collar and cuffs; white and blue checked blouse; felt hat; outfit #064 in the 1955 catalog.

   MARKS: "R&B" (head)
   SEE: *Illustration 103. Sally Herbst Collection.*
   PRICE: $55-75

Littlest Angel Ballerina: HP; 11in (28cm); pink ballerina costume #063; flowers and clip on each side of brunette wig; in 1955 brochure.

   MARKS: "R&B" (head)
   SEE: *Illustration 104. Sally Herbst Collection.*
   PRICE: $55-75

Littlest Angel Bride: HP; 11in (28cm); white bridal gown embroidered all over with tiny flowers; veil of illusion net; carrying a bouquet of white blossoms; #030 in 1955 brochure.

   MARKS: "R&B" (head)
   SEE: *Illustration 105. Sally Herbst Collection.*
   PRICE: $55-75

105.

106.

***Littlest Angel* with Vinyl Head Characteristics:** HP with vinyl head; 11in (28cm); open/closed mouth with detailed molded tongue; molded eyelashes; jointed knees; pin-jointed walker (leg joints with pin hidden under body); sleep eyes with tiny eyelashes painted under the eyes; dimples on back of hands; rooted hair; arm hook (see Identification Guide, page 244). The 1957 brochure listed the vinyl head rooted hair doll for $2.98 and the hard head with foundation wig for $2.59. Both mothers and children preferred the rooted hair dolls.

> MARKS: Marks seen on these dolls:
> "R&B" (head); "R&B Doll
> Company" (body); "11";
> "15"; "16"; "19"; "65";
> "⊥."

***Littlest Angel* in Chinese Costume:** HP with vinyl head; 11in (28cm); purple, gold and black print Chinese-style top with braid; rose pants; small paper umbrella; brunette rooted hair; blue eyes; listed in 1957 brochure as the "R & B Surprise Doll - all packed to go Bye-Bye in her 4 color Gift Box! Dressed 11in *Littlest Angel* Doll. 'Surprise Doll' Book;" 1957. Other Surprise Dolls included English, French, Russian, Italian and Dutch.

> MARKS: Inverted "T" (body); "Littlest Angel BOB #1010" (box)
> SEE: *Illustration 106.*
> PRICE: $75-95 The *Surprise Dolls* are hard to find.

Artisan Doll
(Artisan Novelty Co.)

The registered trademarks, the trademarks and the copyrights appearing in italics within this chapter belong to Artisan.

In 1950 the Artisan Doll Company introduced their new walking doll with a wardrobe of "California Originals" by Michele. Many of the costumes were labeled. The dolls had unusually widespread legs with a heavy walking mechanism. They were very beautiful. The advertisement said, "The dolls could walk, skate, stand alone, and do the splits. Her Ravon wig could be shampooed, combed, and waved." A less expensive doll was the same without the walking mechanism.

MARKS: None (doll); clothes sometimes had a tag
SEE: *Illustration 107. Playthings,* June 1950.
PRICE: $80-110

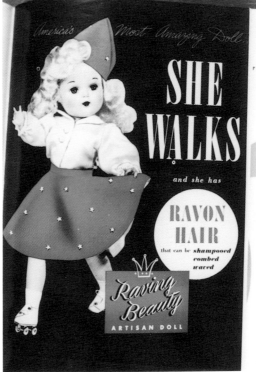

107.

General Characteristics for *Raving Beauty* and *Miss Gadabout:* HP; 20in (51cm); felt tongue with four teeth; wig that could be washed and curled; sleep eyes with real eyelashes; 2nd and 3rd fingers slightly curled; could sit, stand and walk with unusual hip action; Y on seat; 1950. The company made both walkers and non-walkers. (For more information and pictures, see *Hard Plastic Dolls, I,* page 56.)
MARKS: None (doll); clothes sometimes labeled

Raving Beauty: HP; 20in (51cm); (see page 63 for general characteristics). The first wardrobe of "California Originals" by Michele consisted of a square dance costume with brown or blue skirt; cowgirl costume with brown or light blue skirt; skating costume with blue or red gabardine skirt; pastel yellow or blue nightgown with black negligee; black net negligee with black bra and panties; print organdy matinee dress and hat; taffeta wedding gown; all costumes came with accessories; 1950.

    MARKS: None (doll); labels on some of the clothes
    SEE: *Illustration 108. Playthings,* June 1950.
    PRICE: $80-110

Raving Beauty: HP; 100 Series; (see page 63 for general characteristics); doll packed in silver and black tubular container; costumes include #102 sunsuit, #103 playtime costume in white or pastel green, #104 afternoon costume; #101 party costume of light blue taffeta; each costume had panties and shoes; 1950. This doll was not a walking doll. (For further information about Artisan dolls, see *Hard Plastic Dolls, I,* page 56.)

    MARKS: None (doll)
    SEE: *Illustration 109. Playthings,* June 1950.
    PRICE: $100-150

108.

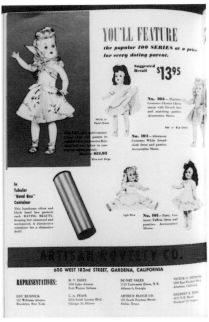

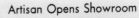

Raving Beauty Walking Doll: HP; 20in (51cm); (see page 63 for general characteristics); early 1950s.

MARKS: None (most dolls)
SEE: *Illustration 110* (doll on left).
Playthings, April 1951.
Illustration 111 (doll on right).
Playthings, August 1951.
PRICE: $100-150

109.

Harry Waters, sales manager for Artisan Dolls, looking mighty pleased with the Raving Beauty Walking Doll, and with the opening of a permanent show room by Artisan at 200 Fifth Ave., New York.

110.

111.

Raving Beauty: HP; 20in (51cm); walking doll; (see page 63 for general characteristics); long yellow formal dress with matching underpants; pinkish satin slippers; tortoise and silver comb in hair; extra outfit of nylon black negligee; early 1950s.

    MARKS: None (doll); "Original Michele//California" (tag on dress); "Raving Beauty//Trademark//Walking Doll//No. 300//Artisan Novelty Company" (box)

    SEE: *Illustration 112. Sharlene Doyle Collection.*

    PRICE: $100-150

112.

Ava Milano Art Doll

The registered trademarks, the trademarks and the copyrights appearing in italics within this chapter belong to Ava Milano Art Doll Company.

Pamela: Italian; HP; 18in (46cm); flirty eyes; human hair wig; individual fingers; painted fingernails; closed mouth; crier box grill; beautiful green organdy dress trimmed with green felt and hand-painted rosebuds; petticoat and separate hooped skirt; pantaloons; leather shoes; matching umbrella; large straw hat; large beautifully printed box. This is an unusually beautiful doll. Both Lenci and Furga were also dressing similar hard plastic dolls in this manner.

    MARKS: "Pamela" (handwritten on head); "AVA//Milano//Art Doll//#35//Extra//Pamela" (box). The signed Pamela on the box and on the head is the same.

    SEE: *Illustration 113. Sandra Strater Collection.*

113. PRICE: $125-150

Baby Barry Toys

The registered trademarks, the trademarks and the copyrights appearing in italics within this chapter belong to Baby Barry Toys.

Baby Barry: HP; 16in (41cm); open mouth with four teeth; felt tongue; braided blonde hair; blue sleep eyes; beige skirt with white blouse; white with blue trimmed suspenders; white shoes, socks and underwear; Y on seat; Wave-A-Doll Hair Kit came with the doll.

MARKS: "Made in USA//170" (back); "Universal Doll Corp.//New York//N.Y." (top of tag); "Style No. 17W//Description//All Hard Plastic//Saran Hair-Wave Kit//Manufactured by//Baby Barry Toys//New York, N.Y." (box); "Wave-A-Doll//Hair//Kit" (box)

SEE: *Illustration 114. Sharlene Doyle Collection.*

114.

PRICE: $50-55

Beddy-Bye and Bye-Bye Doll

The registered trademarks, the trademarks and the copyrights appearing in italics within this chapter belong to Duchess Doll Corp.

Travel Doll: HP; 7¼in (19cm); jointed at neck only; blonde wig; sleep eyes with brown painted lashes above eyes; four fingers molded together; molded painted shoes; included in kit are a gold dress with lace trim; blue flowered print nightgown; pink satin bathrobe; pants; curlers; green felt coat, hat; purse; circa mid 1950s. This company used a *Duchess* doll in their suitcase kit which was made to entertain children while traveling.

MARKS: "DUCHESS DOLL CORP// DESIGN COPYRIGHT //1949" (back of doll)

SEE: *Illustration 115. Marge Meisinger Collection.*

PRICE: $25-30

115.

Belle Doll & Toy Corp.

The registered trademarks, the trademarks and the copyrights appearing in italics within this chapter belong to Belle Doll & Toy Corp. unless otherwise noted.

116.

Saucy Walker® is a registered trademark of the Ideal Toy Corp.

Heddi Stroller: HP; 20in (51cm); head turning walker; Saran pigtail wig; *Saucy Walker*-type; 1952.

> SEE: *Illustration 116. Playthings,* July 1952.
>
> PRICE: $40-50

Bible Doll Co. of America

The registered trademarks, the trademarks and the copyrights appearing in italics within this chapter belong to Bible Doll Co. of America.

David: Very shiny HP; approximately 10in (25cm); raised eyebrows; caracul hair and suit; red belt and boots; came with brochure, "This is David, Your Little Friend From the Bible;" other dolls include Bible characters *Queen Ester, Miriam, Rebekah, Ruth* and *Joseph;* also came with an envelope marked, "Holy Land Earth from the Mount of Olives;" circa mid 1950s.

   SEE: *Illustration 117* (Color Section, page 224). *Eunice Kier Collection.*
   PRICE: Not enough sample prices.

Block Doll Corp.

The registered trademarks, the trademarks and the copyrights appearing in italics within this chapter belong to Block Doll Corp.

The Block Doll Corp. made many dolls for the mass market. Most of them were smaller, inexpensive dolls. They advertised regularly in *Playthings* and not only sold dolls to the public under their name, but they sold to other doll sales companies. Their *Answer Doll* was advertised as early as 1951 and was still advertised in 1957.

For a comparison of some of the collectible "chubby" dolls, see the Identification Guide, page 244.

Answer Doll: HP; 12in (33cm); fully jointed; sleep eyes; nods head "Yes" and shakes head "No." The company advertised that they had other hard plastic miniature dolls with movable parts and sleep eyes that were 5½in (14cm), 6½in (17cm) and 7½in (19cm).

> SEE: *Illustration 118. Playthings,* March 1951.
> PRICE: $45-55 (*Answer Dolls*)   *118.*

Baby Walker: HP; 10½in (27cm); straight leg walker; sleep eyes with molded eyelashes; eyelashes painted under eyes; closed mouth; jointed at neck, shoulders and hips; excellent skin tone; red cheeks and knees; dimples at back of elbows; line above and below knee; double line at front ankle; arm hook (see Identification Guide, page 244); dimples above fingers but not above toes; original clothes; white piqué print with red print roses; snap on dress reads, "Dot Snappers;" unusually nice quality doll; quality of clothing inferior; circa 1955.

> MARKS: None (doll); "Baby Walker// Block Doll Corp." (box)
> SEE: *Illustration 119.*
> PRICE: $45-55

119.

120.

Answer Doll: HP; 12in (31cm); fully jointed; sleep eyes; press back and doll nods "yes;" press tummy and doll nods "no."

> SEE: *Illustration 120. Playthings*, March 1957.

PRICE: $45-55

Chubby-Type: HP; vinyl head; 10½in (27cm); more highly arched eyebrows than Vogue and Arranbee chubby-type dolls; closed mouth; real eyelashes; painted eyelashes under eyes; deep flesh tone; head turning walker; sleep eyes; jointed knees; dimples on elbows; rooted hair; walker; circa 1957.

> MARKS: "Block Doll Product" (head)
> SEE: *Illustration 121. Mary Jane Cultrona Collection*.

PRICE: $30-40

The Central Toy Manufacturing Corporation advertised 3 Block Doll Creations in 1949. These dolls were jointed only at the arms and were among the early inexpensive hard plastic dolls which became so popular. These were advertised "for jobbers and chain stores" and are today good examples of dolls who were made to be sold to other companies. This is one of the reasons so many dolls are hard to research. Unless the purchasing company put on a tag or labeled the box and it stayed with the doll over the years, it is almost impossible to identify. This is true of more expensive dolls also.

> SEE: *Illustration 122. Playthings*, March 1949.

PRICE: $5-6 (as is)

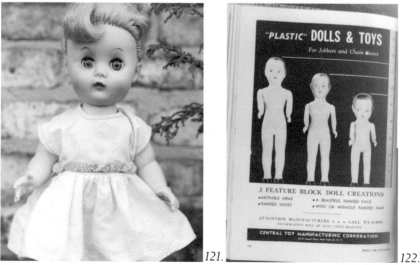

121.

122.

Bonomi Company (Italy)

The registered trademarks, the trademarks and the copyrights appearing in italics within this chapter belong to Bonomi Company.

Annie: HP; sleep eyes with eyelids separate from the eyeballs; lids come down without the eyeballs rolling under; eyes move from side to side; jointed at neck, shoulders and hips; unusual walking mechanism which has instructions, "This doll can walk. Take it by its shoulders or by its waist and push it slowly forward leaning it alternately on one foot and on the other one. In case a leg should unlock from its mechanism, it is enough to make the doll sit down in order that it may be quite ready to walk again. Patented." Instructions were written in Italian, English and German; circa early 1960s.

MARKS: "Bonomi's original doll made in Italy,//Annie" (tag)

SEE: *Illustration 123. Mary Elizabeth Poole Collection.*

PRICE: $85-100

123.

Chiquita Trinkets

The registered trademarks, the trademarks and the copyrights appearing in italics within this chapter belong to Chiquita Trinkets.

These are inexpensive dress-me dolls sold to Chiquita Trinkets of Miami, Florida. They are unusual because they are tropical regional dolls. Dolls pictured include *Tropicana, Hansel* and *Gretel, Rumbera, Miss Muffet* and *Ballerina.* HP; 7½in (19cm); jointed at neck and shoulders; elegantly dressed in lovely organdies, quilted satins, chintzes; trimmed with sea shells and natural foliage; 1951.

MARKS: "An Original//Chiquita Doll//Chiquita Trinkets, Inc. Miami Fla." (bottom of foot)

SEE: *Illustration 124. Playthings,* March 1951.

PRICE: $5-10

124.

Rumbero Doll: HP; 11in (28cm); jointed at neck and shoulders; mohair wig; sleep eyes with light lashes painted above eyes; molded-on shoes (see *Hard Plastic Dolls, I,* page 283A); all original multi-colored costume as shown in advertisement, upper left doll; 1951.

  MARKS: None (doll); "An Original// Chiquita Doll" (tag shaped like a sombrero)
  SEE: *Illustration 125.*
  PRICE: $5-10

125.

Commonwealth Plastics Corp.

The registered trademarks, the trademarks and the copyrights appearing in italics within this chapter belong to Commonwealth Plastics Corp.

Dress-Me Dolls: Commonwealth advertised many different types of undressed dolls throughout the years of 1957 to 1965. Although they were still making hard plastic dolls in various sizes, they advertised in *Playthings* in November of 1959, that they had dolls from 6in (15cm) up. They had, "teen age dolls, adult dolls, baby dolls, boy dolls, colored dolls, vinyl dolls with rooted hair, plastic dolls with dynel, Saran and mohair wigs." They had absorbed the Lingerie Lou Company. (Note the logo in the corner of advertisement.)

  SEE: *Illustration 126. Playthings,* March 1960.

126.

Coronation Hard Plastic Dolls

The coronation of Elizabeth II of England took place in 1953 during the hard plastic doll era. A few of the English souvenir dolls were made of this material by Rosebud and Pedigree.

In the United States souvenir dolls of the coronation were very popular and some hard plastic coronation dolls were produced including the very popular Vogue *Ginny Coronation Doll*® and the lesser known *Beaux Arts Creations*® by Madame Alexander.

The Alexander Doll Company, Inc., catalog of 1953 showed a group of six dolls gracing a miniature spiral staircase. *Queen Elizabeth II* is in the center of the picture and *Princess Margaret Rose* is at the bottom of the stairs. The other four dolls were dressed in wonderful ball gowns with dazzling jewelry and headpieces. The catalog stated, "To own a truly beautiful and elegant doll is certainly the fondest wish of collectors young in heart. Madame Alexander's Beaux Arts Creations are without question the finest dolls ever made. All dolls in this group walk."

Other manufacturers in the United States made less expensive souvenirs, but all of the coronation dolls are colorful, beautiful and very collectible.

Alexander Doll Company

Beaux Arts Creations Queen Elizabeth: HP; 18in (46cm); elaborate white brocade court gown and blue Sash of the Garter; lavishly jeweled tiara, earrings, bracelet; long velvet robe has a cape and border of white fur cloth and silver braid; long white gloves; *Margaret* face; 1953.

> **MARKS:** "Alexander" (doll); "Madame Alexander//All Rights Reserved" New York U.S.A."
> **SEE:** *Illustration 127* (Color Section, page 89).
> **PRICE:** $900-1000 + (very few samples prices available)

Alexander Doll Company

Beaux Arts Creations Princess Margaret Rose: HP; 18in (46cm); blush pink faille taffeta court gown decorated with iridescent sequins; jeweled tiara and bracelet; earrings and necklace are of pearls; long white gloves (not shown); *Margaret* face; 1953.

> **MARKS:** "Alexander" (doll); "Madame Alexander//All Rights Reserved//New York U.S.A."
> **SEE:** *Illustration 128* (Color Section, page 90).
> **PRICE:** $900-1000 + (very few sample prices available)

Ginny® is a registered trademark of Vogue Dolls, Inc.

Beaux Arts Creations®, *Queen Elizabeth*®, *Queen Elizabeth II*®, *Princess Margaret Rose*® and *Margaret*® are registered trademarks of the Alexander Doll Co., Inc.

Alexander Doll Company

Beaux Arts Creations Lady: HP; 18in (46cm); gown of petal soft pink satin; long brocaded satin coat of dove blue trimmed with rhinestone and lined in pink satin; rhinestone tiara (missing) and bracelet; rhinestone earrings; *Margaret* face; 1953. The dove blue satin coat has faded to almost the same color as the pink gown and coat lining. The thread has retained its dove blue color and can be seen upon careful examination. This type of fading often hampers identification for collectors.

    MARKS: "Alexander" (doll); "Madame Alexander//All Rights Reserved//New York U.S.A."

    SEE: *Illustration 129* (Color Section, page 91).

    PRICE: $900-1000 + (very few sample prices available)

Alexander Doll Company

Beaux Arts Creations Lady: HP; 18in (46cm); chartreuse taffeta gown trimmed with rosebuds; big sash of forest green taffeta; gold tiara set with green brilliants; *Margaret* face; 1953. The forest green taffeta has changed to a lovely brown but the green thread can be seen if inspected closely.

    MARKS: "Alexander" (doll); "Madame Alexander//All Rights Reserved//New York U.S.A."

    SEE: *Illustration 130* (Color Section, page 92).

    PRICE: $900-1000 + (very few sample prices available)

Alexander Doll Company

Beaux Arts Creations Lady: HP; 18in (46cm); white satin ball gown; rich red taffeta evening cape; tiny green, faded-to-brown, muff covered with red roses; hair simply arranged with single band of pearls; *Maggie* face; 1953.

    MARKS: "Alexander" (doll); "Madame Alexander//All Rights Reserves//New York U.S.A."

    SEE: *Illustration 131* (Color Section, page 93).

    PRICE: $900-1000 + (very few sample prices available)

Alexander Doll Company

DOLL NOT PHOTOGRAPHED

Beaux Arts Creations Lady: HP; 18in (46cm); youthful gown of aqua taffeta draped with flowing stole of nylon net embroidered with flowers and jewels; jeweled tiara and bracelet; pearl necklace; 1953. (Face unknown.)

Beaux Arts Creations®, *Margaret®* and *Maggie®* are registered trademarks of The Alexander Doll Co., Inc.

Rosebud

Peeress Coronation Doll by L. Reese & Co.: HP; 15in (38cm); non-walker; beautiful brownish-red mohair wig; sleep eyes with real extra long eyelashes; arched eyebrows; eyelashes painted under eyes; molded open mouth and tongue with two tiny painted teeth; very red cheeks like HP English dolls; individual fingers; rather buxom breasts for a child doll; cryer in back with dots in the form of a six-pointed star; well-molded knees; all original heavy cream-colored satin formal dress with slip with crinoline; royal purple robe and royal hat with simulated ermine trim; Cinderella button shoes; 1953.

    MARKS: "Rosebud//Made in England//Pat. No. 667906" (back); "Rosebud" (head)
    SEE: *Illustration 132* (Color Section, page 94).
    PRICE: Not enough samples; very rare doll; seldom seen even in English doll books.

Peeress Coronation Doll® is a registered trademark of L. Reese & Co.

Awin Trading Co. (England)

Coronation Walking Guardsman: HP; 24in (61cm); scarlet tunic; black trousers; belt; bearskin.

Awin was a marketing company which also advertised nylon shirts and boys melton knickers in the same issue of the newspaper.

    SEE: *Illustration 133. Daily Mirror,* May 30, 1953 (England).

Coronation Walking Guardsman® is a registered trademark of the Awin Trading Co.

133.

Pedigree Company Soft Toys, Ltd. (Peter Darling Ltd.)

Coronation Doll: HP; 27in (69cm); hair may be combed; sleep eyes; exquisite flowing robe with sash and golden crown; 1952.

Advertised, "She walks, sits, laughs, recites, sings, and says her prayers in a real human voice." She laughs and says, "He, he, he. I love my mummy. My mummy taught me a rhyme." Says, "Little Bo Peep." Sings, "Oh dear what can the matter be!" Says a prayer.

    Pedigree is known to have sold *Playmate Dolls*. They also used the name Darling for some of their dolls. The advertisement says, "More than a doll — She's a 'Darling' Playmate."

    SEE: *Illustration 134. Daily Mirror,* May 30, 1953 (England).
    PRICE: Not enough sample prices.

Coronation Doll® is a registered trademark of the Peter Darling Ltd.

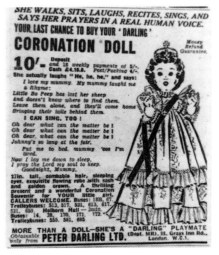

134.

Vogue Dolls, Inc.

Coronation Doll: HP; 8in (20cm); advertisement in *Playthings;* "Queen Elizabeth's Coronation//inspires a//Masterpiece in Miniature; *Ginny,* the Vogue Doll dressed as the Queen of Doll Land..truly Ruler of all the Young in Heart is gowned in a sumptuous white brocaded satin, trimmed with gold and lace. She is wearing the 'Order of the Garter' with a hand-made medallion. Her robe is a majestic sweep of purple velvet trimmed with white fur. Climaxed by a pearl-and golden Crown with scepter is the ultimate in beauty and artistry. A Limited Quantity."

SEE: *Illustration 135. Playthings,* March 1953.

PRICE: $1000 up

135.

Ginny ® is a registered trademark of Vogue Dolls, Inc.

Duchess Doll Corp.

Coronation Doll: HP; 7½in (19cm) and 12½in (32cm); fully jointed; sleep eyes; white-on-white satin dress with lace and gold trim; gold crown; red velveteen cape; advertisement said, "Exquisite likeness of Queen of England." (See *Hard Plastic Dolls, I,* page 86 for picture of the doll.)

MARKS: "Duchess Doll Corp.//Design Copyright//1948" (back of doll)
SEE: *Illustration 136. Playthings,* March 1953.
PRICE: $35-40

Coronation Doll ® is a registered trademark of Duchess Doll Corp.

A and H Doll Mfg. Corp.

Donna Dolls Queen Elizabeth: HP; 12in (31cm); 18 other characters dressed in authentic costume; 1952.

Some doll companies were quick to capitalize on the prospect of the coronation of Princess Elizabeth of England. Long before the actual event, this doll was advertised in *Playthings,* July 1952.

SEE: *Illustration 137. Playthings,* March 1952.
PRICE: $45-50

Queen Elizabeth Doll ® is a registered trademark of the A and H Doll Mfg. Corp.

136.

137.

Doll Bodies (Dolls Of Far-A-Way-Lands, Inc.)

Coronation Doll: HP; 7½in (19cm); also 12in (31cm); jeweled tiara, necklace, bracelet, royal orders; sparkling formal dress of non-tarnishable silver metallic material covered with chantilly lace; royal blue sash; 1953.

SEE: *Illustration 138. Playthings,* March 1953.

PRICE: $35-40

Coronation Doll® is a registered trademark of Doll Bodies, Inc.

Reliable Toy Co. Ltd/Ltee.

Coronation Dolls:

A Little Queen for Coronation Festivities: HP; 8in (20cm); moving eyes; jointed at neck and shoulders only; mohair wig with tiara; colorful coronation robe; beautiful white satin dress with gold trim; painted shoes; ribbon across chest.

A Real Queen in her royal Raiment: HP; 11in (28cm); moving eyes; jointed at neck and shoulders only; dressed in beautiful white satin dress with ribbon and gold trimming; mohair wig with tiara; colorful coronation cape; satin panties; shoes and socks.

Coronation Walking Doll: HP; 12in (31cm); lead her by the hand and she could walk along with you; Saran hair that can be combed, brushed, curled and waved; beautifully dressed in her royal cape and tiara; panties; soft vinyl shoes and socks.

Queen of the Coronation Dolls: HP; 16in (41cm); moving eyes; Saran hair that can be combed, brushed, curled and waved; she could be lead along by the hand and walk; beautifully dressed in white satin with gold trim; royal robe with cape, panties, tiara, socks and soft vinyl shoes.

The above information is from page 15 of the 1953 Reliable catalog.

SEE: *Illustration 139.*

Coronation Doll® is a registered trademark of the Reliable Toy Co. Ltd./Ltee.

138.

139.

Cosmopolitan Doll and Toy Corporation Types of Gingers

Today the Cosmopolitan *Ginger* dolls are widely collected. The collectors in their middle and late thirties remember these wonderful dolls who were very affordable. Like many of the small walking dolls, they had an extensive wardrobe and a wide variety of accessories. The sizes of the dolls ranged from 7½in (19cm) to 8½in (22cm). During the days of their manufacture, there were changes in their body styles to keep up with the latest innovations in doll technology.

An extensive study of *Ginger* characteristics and *Ginger* body styles can be found in the Identification Guide, page 238-239. Other information can be found in *Hard Plastic Dolls, I*, page 81.

Variations in the *Ginger*-type all-HP dolls include:

1. Early painted eyelash, straight leg non-walkers and walkers (see page 238).
2. Large sleep eye, straight leg walkers (see page 238).
3. Medium sleep eye, straight leg walkers (see page 238).
4. Small sleep eye, straight leg walkers (see page 238).
5. Bent knee walkers (see page 238, 239).
6. Bent knee and bent elbow walkers (see page 238).
7. Dolls with black flesh tone.

Ginger dolls with HP bodies and vinyl heads include:

1. Rooted hair, straight leg walkers (see page 238).
2. Rooted hair, straight leg walkers with Cha Cha heels (see page 238).

For pictures of the various body types see, Identification Guide page 238-239.

Most of the *Ginger* dolls had blue eyes but some dolls had green, brown and lavender eyes. These last dolls also had lavender hair.

The following marketing companies used one of the basic *Gingers:*

1. Terri Lee dressed them in Scout and Brownie Uniforms. (See *Hard Plastic Dolls, I*, page 82, *Illustration 186*).
2. Active *Mindy*
3. Midwestern *Mary Jean* (See page 150.)
4. Marcelle Boissier *Jeanette*
5. Admiration Girl (See page 17.) These are late dolls made in Hong Kong and have unusual arms and lightweight hard plastic.
6. Companies who made regional souvenirs.
7. Advertising dolls of various kinds including a perfume and cosmetic company who sold a Spanish doll.

Often the dolls sold to other companies had the large eyes and an inferior hard plastic. These were sold under different names.

Ginger not only had a large wardrobe, her accessories, furniture and books included:

---

1. Trunks and luggage
2. Hats
3. Stands and hangers
4. Wigs
5. Ice skates, roller skates and extra shoes
6. House, patio and lawn furniture
7. Wardrobes for clothing
8. Gift sets (See *Hard Plastic Dolls, I,* page 82, *Illustrations 183* and *184.*)
9. Cardboard doll house
10. *Little Golden Book* about *Ginger*
11. Packaged *Ginger* clothes that came to members of the *Ginger* "Doll of the Month Club"

Cosmopolitan also had permission to use costumes related to Disney characters and Disneyland. (See *Illustrations 146-148.*)

Other types of *Ginger* dolls made by Cosmopolitan include:
1. *Ginger Baby.*
2. *Miss Ginger* (See *Glamour Dolls of the 1950s & 1960s,* pages 81-84.)
3. *Little Miss Ginger* (See *Glamour Dolls of the 1950s & 1960s,* page 84.)

Painted Eye Ginger Nurse: HP; 8in (20cm); early doll with painted eyelashes above eyes; straight leg walker; medium eyes (see Identification Guide, *Illustration 421*); dressed as nurse in marked *Ginger* costume; circa 1954. Later painted eye *Gingers* came as jointed knee walkers.

MARKS: None (doll); "Fashions for 'Ginger'//Cosmopolitan Doll & Toy Corp.// Jackson Heights, N.Y." (tag sewn into uniform)

SEE: *Illustration 140. Pat Parton Collection.*

PRICE: $45-50

Ginger: HP; 8in (20cm); walker; sleep eyes; advertisement said, "The only eight inch walking doll with a fully lined and stitched Saran wig." The extra outfits were boxed with shoes and socks; 1955 wardrobe.

SEE: *Illustration 141. Playthings,* August 1955.

140.

141.

142.

143.

Ginger in Mexican Outfit: as shown in advertisement in *Playthings*, March 1955; cotton jumpsuit; white cotton blouse; matching straw hat with pompon trim; cowboy boots.

    MARKS: None (doll)

    SEE: *Illustration 142. Marge Meisinger Collection.*

    PRICE: $55-75+

Mousketeers: HP; advertised as "The only doll in the Mickey Mouse Club;" from left to right: *Ginger* in her Mickey Mouse Sweater Costume; *Ginger* in her Mousekarade Costume; *Ginger* in her official *Talent Roundup Costume;* vinyl *Mickey Mouse* mask included with each outfit; 1955.

    SEE: *Illustration 143. Playthings,* September 1955.

    PRICE: $75-100+ (very few sample prices available)

Ginger in Mouseketeer Mousekarade Costume: red jersey suit with Mickey Mouse patch; black belt, boots and cap with Mickey Mouse ears; 1955.

    MARKS: None (doll)

    SEE: *Illustration 144* (Color Section, page 167). *Marge Meisinger Collection.*

    PRICE: $75-100+ (very few sample prices available)

Ginger in Mouseketeer Official Talent Roundup Costume: blue felt skirt with white felt trim; blue top; white cowboy hat; cowboy boots; 1955.

   MARKS: None (doll)

   SEE: *Illustration 145. Marge Meisinger Collection.*

   PRICE: $75-100+ (very few sample prices available)

145.

Ginger visits Adventureland in Disneyland:
1. *Cha-Cha-Cha Seniorita*
2. *Safari Girl*
3. *Oriental Princess*
   SEE: *Illustration 146.* Ginger brochure, 1956.

Trousseau Series:
1. *Bride*
2. *Bridesmaid*
3. *Bridesmaid*
   SEE: *Illustration 146.* Ginger brochure, 1956.

146.

Ginger Visits Frontierland in Disneyland:
1. *Indian Princess*
2. *Frontier Girl*
3. *Pioneer Girl*

Ginger Visits Fantasyland in Disneyland:
1. *Blue Fairy*
2. *Cinderella*
3. *Dream Princess*
   SEE: *Illustration 147.* Ginger brochure, 1956.

147.

148.

Ginger Visits Tomorrowland in Disneyland:
1. *Rocket Pilot*
2. *Sun Princess*
3. *Space Girl*

Ginger Visits the Mickey Mouse Club:
1. *Mousekarade Costume*
2. *Official Treatment Roundup Costume*
3. *Official Mickey Mouse Club Costume*
   SEE: *Illustration 148.* Ginger brochure, 1956.

Ginger Gay Nineties Series:
1. Long dress with fur stole; doll has upswept hair.
2. Long dress with three ruffles on the skirt; embroidery trim on bottom of each ruffle; wide dark hat; dark hair.
3. Long dress with three net ruffles on skirt; light wide hat with feather trim; blonde hair.
   SEE: *Illustration 149.* Ginger brochure, 1956.

Ginger Activity Series: left to right

Upper row	Lower Row
1. Ice skating costume	1. Beach clothes
2. Roller skating costume	2. Drum majorette uniform
3. Ballerina tutu	3. Fireman uniform

SEE: *Illustration 149.* Ginger brochure, 1956.

149.

Ginger Ballerina: HP; 7½in (19cm); *Ginger* characteristics (see Identification Guide, page 238); slightly different arm hook (see Identification Guide, page 238) and jointed elbows; yellow ballerina outfit; circa 1956-1957. The same doll was pictured in *Hard Plastic Dolls, I,* Unknown Section, page 234.

MARKS: None (doll); "Fashions for Ginger Cosmopolitan Doll and Toy Company" (tag on dress)

SEE: *Illustration 150.*
PRICE: $35-40

150.

Cha Cha Heel Ginger: HP; vinyl head; 8in (20cm); *Ginger* characteristics (see Identification Guide, page 238) except for legs; head turning walker but legs have been restyled with medium heels; head has unusually nice vinyl with lovely color; sleep eyes operate smoothly; 1957.

This doll is rare because Cosmopolitan also introduced the high-heeled *Little Miss Ginger* on the right in the illustration. She was much more popular with the children.

MARKS: "Ginger" (bottom of feet and shoes)
SEE: *Illustration 151.*
    Illustration 152. Playthings, March 1957.
PRICE: $35-50+ (very few sample prices available)

151.

152.

153.

Ginger and Miss Ginger: advertisement in *Playthings,* March 1957; *Ginger* is HP; *Miss Ginger* is approximately 10in (25cm); vinyl; matching outfits for *Ginger* and her Slim Teen Age Sister; *Miss Ginger's* dresses came with silk stockings, high-heeled shoes and jewelry.

> SEE: *Illustration 153. Playthings,* March 1957.
>
> PRICE: $40-55 (*Ginger*)
> $40-55 (*Miss Ginger*)

Ginger Doll-Mate: promotion used in 1957 to sell more *Ginger* dolls and clothes. *Ginger* Doll-ers were given with the purchases. The customer could send five *Ginger* Doll-ers plus one real dollar ($1) plus a child's picture and she would receive a *Ginger* DOLL-MATE which could be dressed in any of *Ginger's* beautiful outfits. This was a masonite cut out doll in real lifelike color with the child's picture pasted on it.

> SEE: *Illustration 154. Playthings,* March 1957.

154.

D & D Mfg. Co.

Nun: HP; 12in (31cm); non-walking; Plastic Molded Arts characteristics (see *Hard Plastic Dolls, I* page 207); molded-on shoes painted white (see Identification Guide, *Hard Plastic Dolls, I*, page 283, *Illustration 612*); black taffeta nun's habit with rosary beads and cross at the waist. Printing on box says, "Attend Church regularly...//for the Family that Prays Together...Stays Together!" 1954.

MARKS: None (doll); "No. 1400 Nun Doll//1954 D & D MFG. Co." (box)

SEE: *Illustration 155.*

PRICE: $25-30

155.

A. H. Delfausse Company

Mademoiselle: HP; walking doll; no height given in advertisement; toddler doll; has wardrobe; 1953.

SEE: *Illustration 156. Playthings,* March 1953.

PRICE: $25-30

156.

De Soto
Manufacturing Company

The registered trademarks, the trademarks and the copyrights appearing in italics within this chapter belong to De Soto Manufacturing Company.

157.

Randy Goes to the Circus: HP head; no other information available.

> **SEE:** *Illustration 157. Playthings,* March 1950.
> **PRICE:** $25-40

Diamont (Germany)

The registered trademarks, the trademarks and the copyrights appearing in italics within this chapter belong to Diamont.

Boy in Lederhosen: HP; 14in (36cm); molded hair under human hair wig; sleep eyes with real eyelashes; unusual closed mouth with deep indentation under chin; dimples on knees and elbows; jointed at neck, shoulders and hips; chubby body; black Bavarian hat; blue pants and red print shirt; cobbled leather shoes; circa mid 1950s. This doll has a wonderful character face which lends itself to the typical type of German hard plastic used in that country.

> **MARKS:** "Diamont" in oval (head)
> **SEE:** *Illustration 158. Shirley Niziolek Collection.*
> **PRICE:** $85-110

158.

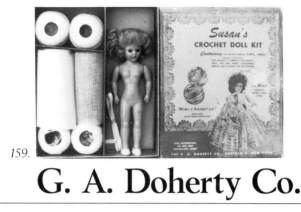

159.

G. A. Doherty Co.

The registered trademarks, the trademarks and the copyrights appearing in italics within this chapter belong to G. A. Doherty Co.

Susan's Crochet Doll Kit: HP; 7in (18cm); Duchess doll is used in the kit made by G. A. Doherty Co.; Duchess characteristics (see page 99); kit has materials to make a crocheted bride dress with satin, flowers, ribbon and D.M.C. crochet thread which were included in the kit; circa 1948-1950.

    MARKS: "Duchess Doll Corp.//Design Copyright//1948" (back)
    SEE: *Illustration 159.*
    PRICE: $12-15

Doll Bodies, Inc. (Originally Lingerie Lou)

The registered trademarks, the trademarks and the copyrights appearing in italics within this chapter belong to Doll Bodies, Inc., unless otherwise noted.

Mary-Lu Walker: HP; 18in (46cm); walking doll; sleep eyes; painted eyelashes under eyes; ponytail or pigtail Dynel hair that is washable, brushable and combable; an assortment of 16 different dresses could be purchased for her or another 18in (46cm); 1955.

    SEE: *Illustration 160. Playthings,*
        March 1955 (top).
    PRICE: $40-45

160.

Mary-Lu: HP; 7¼in (19cm); Dynel hair that can be washed, combed and set; came with panties in a heat-sealed package; clothes could be purchased separately; walking doll with same characteristics as the Roberta doll; molded and painted shoes with bows in front (see Identification Guide, *Hard Plastic Dolls, I,* page 286K); fatter legs than most of the *Ginny*-type dolls; 1955.

    MARKS: None
    SEE: *Illustration 160. Playthings,* March 1955 (bottom).
    PRICE: $6-12

Ginny® is a registered trademark of Vogue Dolls, Inc.

Continued on page 97.

Alexander 1953 Beaux Arts Creations, No. 2025, *Queen Elizabeth II* (see page 73).

Alexander 1953 Beaux Arts Creations, No. 2020B, *Princess Margaret Rose* (see page 73).

Alexander 1953 Beaux Arts Creations, No. 2020C, Lady (see page 74).

Alexander 1953 Beaux Arts Creations, No. 2020E, Lady (see page 74).

Alexander 1953 Beaux Arts Creations, No. 2020F, Lady (see page 74).

Rosebud (England) *Peeress Coronation* (see page 75).

Alexander pink *Bride* (see page 19).

Alexander *Elise Renoir* (see page 29).

American Character, page from company catalog, *Sweet Sue* (see page 47).

Arranbee *Nancy Lee* (see page 51). *Lois Janner Collection.*

Continued from page 88.

161.

Mary-Lu Walker: HP; 16in (41cm); open mouth with four teeth; sleep eyes with real lashes; lashes also painted under the eyes; excellent flesh tone; shiny hard plastic; all original; turquoise dress with white organdy collar; circa 1955.

> **MARKS:** "A Product of Doll Bodies Inc. New York 12, N.Y." (box); None (doll).
> **SEE:** *Illustration 161. Ruth M. Casey Collection.*
> **PRICE:** $50-60 (in box)

Dress-Me Dolls: HP; various sizes from 7½in (19cm) to 11½in (29cm); sleep eyes; some fully jointed; others jointed only at neck and shoulders; mohair wigs; packaged in heat-treated cellophane envelopes; 1955. These dolls were sold well into the 1960s, and they were packaged in many ways. Often they came with as many as 16 sewing patterns complete with sewing instructions. Some came with a 16-page book of colored pictures of costumes of all nations. Stands were also available.

> **MARKS:** Usually none
> **SEE:** *Illustration 162. Playthings,* March 1955.
> **PRICE:** $5-15

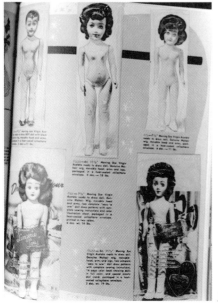

162.

Dress-me Doll: HP; 7½in (19cm); doll in plastic bra and pants; sewing kit with two dolls, two stands and two patterns, *Lingerie Lou's Doll Collection Book.*

    MARKS: None (doll)

    SEE: *Illustration 163. Playthings,* August 1952.

    PRICE: $12-15

Dolls of Faraway Lands: HP; authentically costumed dolls in satins, braids and taffetas; sleep eyes; jointed head and arms only; 1953. These dolls were advertised for collectors. They were packaged in gift window boxes and sold by Dolls of Far-A-Way Lands, Inc., a subsidiary of Doll Bodies, Inc.

    MARKS: "Dolls of Faraway Lands" (boxes)

    SEE: *Illustration 164. Playthings,* March 1953.

    PRICE: $5-10

163.

164.

Duchess Doll Corp.

The registered trademarks, the trademarks and the copyrights appearing in italics within this chapter belong to Duchess Doll Corp.

Duchess was a very active company during the hard plastic era. They not only sold dolls under their name, but they sold dolls to other companies which were used in unusual and attractive kits to keep children busy and happy. (See G. A. Doherty Co., page 88 and Beddy-Bye and Bye-Bye Doll Company, page 67.)

Duchess Small Doll Characteristics: HP; 7in (18cm) to 8in (20cm); side-glancing or sleep eyes; painted, molded Virga-type shoes (see Identification Guide, *Hard Plastic Dolls, I*, page 284D); inexpensive clothing which was usually stapled on; 1st, 2nd, 3rd and 4th fingers molded together; arm hook (see Identification Guide, *Hard Plastic Dolls, I*, page 268V). The company was famous for their boxed "International Series" which was often given as a bonus at the local grocery store. They made other boxed dolls. They are very collectible today.

Dale Evans: HP; 8in (29cm); jointed at arms only; white cowgirl suit made of plastic; red plastic cuffs; red felt gun holster; gold buckle; white felt hat; white boots; clothes stapled onto doll; Virga-type shoes (see Identification Guide, *Hard Plastic Dolls, I*, page 285H); circa 1948.

 MARKS: "Duchess Doll Corp.// Design Copyright//1948" (back)
 SEE: *Illustration 165.*
 PRICE: $15-20

165.

166.

Miss Valentine of 1951: HP; 7-1/2in (19cm); dress is a white and red printed rayon gown trimmed with ribbon and decorated with gold braid; packaged in an acetate window box.

> MARKS: "Duchess Doll Corp.// Design Copyright//1948" (back)
> SEE: *Illustration 166. Playthings*, December 1951.
> PRICE: $15-20

Peter Pan and Tinker Bell: HP; 7in (18cm); Walt Disney characters 1st, 2nd, 3rd and 4th fingers molded together. This was made and advertised to take advantage of the movie *Peter Pan* which was released that year; 1953.

> MARKS: "Duchess Doll Corp// Design Copyright//1948" (back)
> SEE: *Illustration 167. Playthings*, May 1953.
> PRICE: $15-20 each

167.

Alice in Wonderland: HP; 12-1/2in (32cm) and 7-1/2in (19cm); sleep eyes; jointed at neck, shoulders and hips; issued in a "Dolls of all Nations" box; 1951. Walt Disney's production of *Alice in Wonderland* was released in August 1951. Other Disney characters by Duchess include *Cinderella* in 12-1/2in (32cm) and 7-1/2in (19cm) sizes and *Snow White* in the 7-1/2in (19cm) size only.

    MARKS: None (doll)
    SEE: *Illustration 168. Playthings*, August 1951.
    PRICE: $20-30

Italian Dream Girl: HP; 13in (33cm); blue sleep eyes with lashes; brunette wig; jointed at neck, legs and arms; arm hook (see Identification Guide, *Hard Plastic Dolls, I*, page 267S); painted, molded shoes (see Identification Guide, *Hard Plastic Dolls, I*, page 285I); 1st, 2nd and 3rd fingers molded together; red satin skirt; white organdy apron, blouse, scarf; carrying a small basket with a chick inside; excellent quality hard plastic; circa 1952. The doll in *Hard Plastic Dolls, I* on page 103, *Illustration 240, Violetta*, is also a Duchess doll.

    MARKS: None (doll); "A Duchess Dream Girl Doll - Italian" (box)
    SEE: *Illustration 169.*
    PRICE: $25

168.

169.

170.

Duchess advertised in 1953 that they had a new picture frame box. "This new Duchess DeLuxe Series brings to you the same incomparable Duchess Doll packaged in a real Picture Frame Box. The Picture Frame enables you to hang the Duchess Doll on the wall and also to stand it on a display counter by means of a built-in easel..."

SEE: *Illustration 170. Playthings,* March 1953.

PRICE: $15-20

Eegee (Goldberger Doll Mfg. Co., Inc.)

The registered trademarks, the trademarks and the copyrights appearing in italics within this chapter belong to Goldberger Doll Mfg. Co., Inc.

Gigi Perreau: HP body and vinyl head; 20in (51cm); Dynel rooted washable hair; fully-jointed body; open mouth with teeth; Ninon dress; 1952. Gigi Perreau was a Universal-International starlet. Eegee promised dealers a promotional package which included personal appearances with Gigi Perreau, theater tie-ins from coast-to-coast, free photo prints with the doll and free newspaper mats.

SEE: *Illustration 171. Playthings,* September 1952.

PRICE: $65-100

171.

Susan Stroller: HP; 23in (58cm); head turning walker; Saran hair with curlers; sleep eyes; crying mama voice; sleep eyes; 1953.

    MARKS: "Eegee" (head); "EE-GEE" (body); or none

    SEE: *Illustration 172. Playthings,* February 1953.

    PRICE: $50-55

172.

Effanbee Doll Corp.

The registered trademarks, the trademarks and the copyrights appearing in italics within this chapter belong to Effanbee Doll Corp.

173.

Howdy Doody: HP heads and hands; stuffed cloth body; 23in (58cm); 19in (48cm); sleep eyes; molded hair; dressed in cowboy costume with scarf with "Howdy Doody" on it; 1947-1949.

    MARKS: *"Effanbee"* (head)

    SEE: *Illustration 173. Playthings,* March 1949.

    PRICE: $150-200 19in (48cm)
                 $200-250 23in (58cm)

174.

Electronic Doll: 28in (71cm); jointed at neck, shoulders and hips; sings, laughs, talks and says her prayers in a human voice when you press the button; sings, "London Bridge's Falling Down" and "Mary Had a Little Lamb;" says, "Now I Lay Me Down to Sleep;" pink dress with black and white checked trim; 1950.

> SEE: *Illustration 174.* Advertisement for Effanbee Dolls...a Division of Noma Electric Corp.
>
> PRICE: $125-175+ (very few sample prices available)

By the early 1950s doll wardrobes became very important. Dress designers in France and the United States also designed beautiful doll clothes for many different types of dolls. Madame Schiaparelli designed doll clothes for her daughter, Gogo, and Effanbee persuaded her to design a collection of clothes for their *Honey* doll. These dolls were limited to America's finest stores on a franchise basis. Only one franchise was allowed in a city. At that time Effanbee was a division of Noma Electric Corp.

> SEE: *Illustration 175. Playthings,* July 1951.

175.

Schiaparelli Doll: HP; 18in (46cm); close-fitting blonde wig; sleep eyes; jointed at neck, shoulders and hips; walker; beautiful flesh color; pink embossed organdy with darker pink roses; black shoes; white socks; *Honey Walker* mold; 1951. (Costume may not be original.)

    MARKS: "Effanbee" (back)

    SEE: *Illustration 176. Ester Borgis Collection.*

    PRICE: $250-325 + depending on costume (rare doll — very few sample prices)

Tintair Honey: HP; 16in (41cm); sleep eyes; red coloring on knees and back of hand; jointed at neck, arms and legs; blonde hair (almost white); turquoise glazed waffle dress with white organdy sleeves and yoke trimmed in eyelet organdy; pink shoes; pink bows in hair; all original; boxed set includes "Glossy Chestnut" and "Carrot Top" non-poisonous hair color; applicator; curlers; 1951.

    MARKS: "Effanbee" (neck); "I am the Tintair Doll (4 curlers) An Effanbee Durable Doll" (tag front); "A New Effanbee Playmate//May You and your Tintair Dolly have many happy times together// Trademark Reg//Made in U.S." (tag back)

    SEE: *Illustration 177* (doll in box, Color Section, page 163).

    Illustration 178 (advertisement). *Playthings,* August 1951.

    PRICE: $225-300 + (as pictured in box)

176.

Every little girl's

EFFANBEE DOLL CO.

178.

Honey Bride: HP; 14in (36cm); head turning walker; sleep eyes with real eyelashes; jointed at neck, shoulders and hips; red headed wig; all original satin bride dress with full skirt ending in a graceful train; looped fringe trim around a flattering shawl; bib collar; taffeta petticoat over crinoline; taffeta panties; white satin slippers; 1952.

   MARKS: "Effanbee" (head); "Effanbee" (back)
   SEE: *Illustration 179* (Color Section, page 166).
   PRICE: $170-200 14in (36cm)
              $180-225 16in (41cm) depending on costume
              $195-240 18in (46cm) depending on costume
              $275-325 24in (61cm) depending on costume

Honey Walker Ice Skater: HP; 18in (46cm); sleep eyes; jointed at neck, shoulders and hips; beautiful skin color; all original white skating costume; fur capelet and muff; 1951-1953.

   MARKS: Effanbee (back); "Honey Walker" (box and tag)
   SEE: *Illustration 180. Gigi Williams Collection.*
   PRICE: $195-240

180.

Elite Creations

The registered trademarks, the trademarks and the copyrights appearing in italics within this chapter belong to Elite Creations, unless otherwise noted.

Vicki: HP; 8in (20cm); facial characteristics and tubular arm hooks of the *Pam*® doll (see *Hard Plastic Dolls, I,* Identification Guide, page 2660); does not have the molded slippers of *Pam*®; the toes have excellent detail with dimples above toes; jointed at neck, shoulders, hips and knees; red, black and yellow plaid shirt; blue jeans; red shoes; brown pigtails; (see body construction, Identification Guide, page 239); mid 1950s.

   MARKS: None (doll); "Elite Creations" (brochure)
   SEE: *Illustration 181. Ester Borgis Collection.*
   PRICE: $30-40

Pam® is a registered trademark of Fortune Toys, Inc.

181.

Brochure with Doll: from left to right:
1. Roller skating outfit with dark print skirt and white top; roller skates.
2. Tennis outfit; shorts and top; tennis racket.
3. Jeans and shirt shown on doll in picture.
4. Nurse's uniform.
Poem on Right Side of Doll
"To make your Vicki doll look smart
Select her wardrobe from this chart
Run over to your local store
Don't leave before you see some more."
    SEE: *Illustration 181. Ester Borgis Collection.*

Vicki **Brochure:**
    SEE: *Illustration 182. Ester Borgis Collection.*
    PRICE: $5-10 (individual outfit in box)

182.

183.

Vicki **Brochure:**
    SEE: *Illustration 183. Ester Borgis Collection.*
    PRICE: $5-10 (individual outfit in box)

| No. 402 BRIDESMAID | No. 401 BRIDE | No. 407 PINAFORE | No. 403 HAT AND COAT | No. 412 BALLERINA | No. 405 PARTY DRESS |

184.

Vicki Brochure: right hand picture only:
1. Bride in white rayon dress with net veil.
2. Bridesmaid in pink rayon dress with flower in hair.
   SEE: *Illustration 184. Ester Borgis Collection.*
   PRICE: $5-10 (individual outfit in box)

Eugenia Doll Company, Inc.

The registered trademarks, the trademarks and the copyrights appearing in italics within this chapter belong to Eugenia Doll Company, Inc., unless otherwise noted.

Pam, the Perm-O-Wave Doll: HP; 14in (36cm); human hair wig which could be set in any style with the popular Perm-O-Wave curlers; the curlers could also be used to give home permanents to the mother and daughter; included also a plastic makeup cape, comb, barrette and carrying case; 1949. This was one of the earliest home permanent dolls.
   SEE: *Illustration 185. Playthings,* April 1949.

185.

Doll in Child's Dress: HP; 18in (46cm); (for general characteristics, see *Illustration 187*); organdy dress with lace trim; 1947-1949.

> **MARKS:** None (doll); "A Personality// Play-Mate" (box)
> **SEE:** *Illustration 186. Betty Shriver Collection.*
> **PRICE:** $150-175

Doll in Pink Dress in Box: HP; 18in (46cm); beautiful wig; feathered eyebrows; sleep eyes with five lines painted at each side of eye; nail polish; 2nd and 3rd fingers molded together and slightly curved; body similar to *Nancy Ann Style Show* doll; red on knees and hands; wide Y on seat; pink organdy dress with circular fluted hat; 1947-1949.

> **MARKS:** None (doll); "A Personality// Play-Mate" (box)
> **SEE:** *Illustration 187. Sherry Dempsey Collection.*
> **PRICE:** $150-175

Nancy Ann Style Show® is a registered trademark of Nancy Ann Storybook Dolls, Inc.

187.

186.

Juliette Bridal Doll: HP; 21in (53cm); human hair wig; jointed at neck, shoulders and hips; closed mouth; 1947.

    SEE: *Illustration 188. Playthings,* March 1947.

    PRICE: $175-200

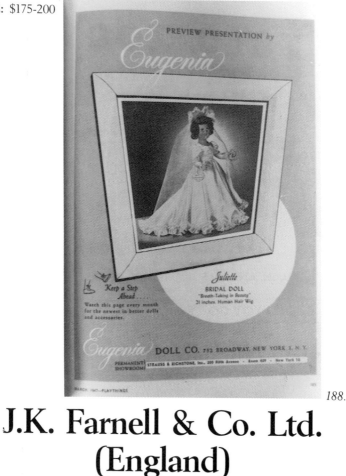

188.

J.K. Farnell & Co. Ltd. (England)

The registered trademarks, the trademarks and the copyrights appearing in italics within this chapter belong to J.K. Farnell & Co. Ltd.

Plastic Dolls: HP; various sizes; dolls were made through the 1960s and possibly into the 1970s. Small girl and boy dolls were sold to sales companies who costumed a line of souvenir dolls such as soldiers, Scottish dolls, Welsh dolls, and so forth.

The Farnell company made a line of Alpha Toys. In the 1930s they made cloth dolls which were similar to Chad Valley or Norah Wellings dolls. They used the trademark names of *Joy Day* and *Alpha Cherub Dolls.*

    MARKS: "Alpha" (back) on some of the hard plastic dolls; none on other dolls

Fleischaker Novelty Company

The registered trademarks, the trademarks and the copyrights appearing in italics within this chapter belong to Fleischaker Novelty Company.

Little Girl of Today: HP body; head, arms and legs made of soft plastic which feels like real flesh; molded hair doll is 22in (56cm); rooted hair doll is 22in (56cm) and 28in (71cm); rooted human hair; glassine eyes; talks and walks when guided; dressed in organdy dress with matching one available for little girls; pictures of hair styles for the doll and hairdressing tips were available in an accompanying brochure; 1951.

This was a very early rooted hair doll.

   SEE: *Illustration 189. Playthings,* June 1951.
       Illustration 190. Playthings, June 1951.

189.

190.

Fortune Toys Incorporated

The registered trademarks, the trademarks and the copyrights appearing in italics within this chapter belong to Fortune Toys Incorporated, unless otherwise noted.

One of the most popular dolls sold by Fortune Toys Incorporated was a small walking doll which competed with *Ginny*®. Although the dolls had the same characteristics, they were sold as *Pam, Ninette* and *Starlet, the Lustercreme Doll*. There may have been others also sold under the Fortune name. Fortune was connected with Beehler Arts and Ontario Plastics.

Virga was also another company connected with Beehler Arts and Ontario Plastics. They sold dolls with the same characteristics called *Lucy*®, *Schiaparelli GoGo*®, *Lolly Pop*®, *Play-Mates*®, *Play-Pals*® and others.

Kim, another company, used the same address as Beehler Arts on their dolls' boxes. These dolls were called *Kim*.

Other dolls with the same characteristics were sold by Doll Bodies, Grant Plastics, Niresk Industries, Plastic Molded Arts, Roberta Dolls and Norma Dolls.

There is a difference in the quality of both the hard plastic and the costuming of these dolls. For more information and pictures of these dolls, see the Identification Guide, page 242. It is difficult to know which company sold a doll originally unless it has a tag or is in a marked box.

The following characteristics are common to all these dolls:
1. 7½in (19cm) to 8in (20cm) in height. However, a few are as tall as 9in (23cm). (See *Illustration 366* in the Virga section.)
2. Tube-like arm hook (see Identification Guide, *Hard Plastic Dolls, I*, page 266O).
3. Molded-on T-strap shoes (seen Identification Guide of this book, page 252I).
4. Sleep eyes.
5. Crease in center of kneecap.
6. Seamline cut through the back part of ear.
7. Many with molded hair under wig.
8. Deep indentation under lower lip (no dimple).
9. 2nd and 3rd fingers molded together.

The Fortune company made other types of dolls which are shown in *Hard Plastic Dolls, I*, pages 241-244.

Ninette: HP; 8in (20cm) head turning small walking doll; 24 outfits available; 1955. This doll competed with *Ginny*®.
Clothes shown in advertisement include:

1. *Morning dress*	9. *Clown outfit*
2. *Spring dress*	10. *Majorette outfit*
3. *Bridal dress*	11. *Halloween outfit*
4. *Cowgirl outfit*	12. *Little Miss Muffet*
5. *School dress*	13. *Formal dance gown*
6. *Lounging ensemble*	14. *Red ensemble*
7. *Garden outfit*	15. *Party dress*
8. *Ski outfit*	

MARKS: None (body)
SEE: *Illustration 191. Playthings*, April 1955.
PRICE: $25-30

191.

See *Illustration 192* on page 139.

Pam: The box for the *Pam* doll advertised "Michele Cartier//presents//Pam//and// her fabulous wardrobe." For pictures of *Pam* dolls, see pages 101 and 102, *Hard Plastic Dolls, I.* The individual clothing boxes which could be purchased separately were inscribed with the same words.

    MARKS: None (doll)
    SEE: *Illustration 193. Marge Meisinger Collection.*
    PRICE: $30-35 (doll)

193.

G.H. & E. Freydberg, Inc.

The registered trademarks, the trademarks and the copyrights appearing in italics within this chapter belong to G.H. & E. Freydberg, Inc, unless otherwise noted.

Mary Jane: HP; 17in (43cm); made in imitation of *Terri Lee®*; closed mouth that is wider than *Terri Lee®*; flirty eyes; eyebrows more arched than *Terri Lee®*; painted eyelashes on side of eye; redder flesh color and more glossy than *Terri Lee®*; head turns as it walks; 2nd and 3rd fingers molded together; more slender body than *Terri Lee®*; sleep eyes; doll dressed in bright pink dress with lace trim; green pajamas; green, brown and white checked robe; checked shirt and jeans; 1953.

    MARKS: None (doll); "Mary Jane" (tag sewn into clothes)
    SEE: *Illustration 194.*
    PRICE: $150-175

194.

Terri Lee® is a registered trademark of the Terri Lee Dolls, Inc.

Mary Jane: two pages of advertising the doll and her clothing; 1953. SEE: *Illustration 195. Playthings,* June 1953.

195.

Furga (Italy)

The registered trademarks, the trademarks and the copyrights appearing in italics within this chapter belong to Furga.

Girl in Blue Dress: Italian HP; 14in (36cm); dark skin tone; blonde wig; sleep eyes with long Italian (very long) lashes; feathered eyebrows; two-toned pink lips; jointed at neck, shoulders and hips; all original; blue rayon long dress and matching hat with pink trim; cotton teddy; circa mid 1950s.

MARKS: "Furga" (head); "Made in Itali" (stamped on chest); "Made in Italy" (tag sewn into clothes)

SEE: *Illustration 196. Jill Kaar Collection.*

PRICE: $125-150

196.

Grant Plastics, Inc.

A few of the doll companies of the 1950s specialized in the "Dress-Me" type dolls. A handful actually did the manufacturing. Others acted as national wholesalers and sold to companies who dressed the dolls. They also sold to regional wholesalers who in turn sold in smaller lots to doll shops, doll hospitals and to local people who wanted to dress a few to sell for profit or sell at a bazaar. Even today similar dolls made of vinyl can be found in the local craft shops.

Grant Plastics, Inc., advertised in *Playthings* magazine and their line was extensive.

Marcia: HP; 7½in (19cm); sleep eyes; jointed at neck and shoulders; two easy-to-sew patterns included with a complete 16-page colored booklet of simple sewing instructions; painted shoes; doll stand included; packed in heat-sealed poly bag; one of the *Adorable Dress-Me Dolls*; circa 1959-1963.

MARKS: None (doll)
SEE: *Illustration 197* (doll on left).
    Playthings, March 1961.
PRICE: $5-10

Sylvia: HP with vinyl head; 18in (47cm); walking doll; rooted hair; jointed at neck, shoulders and hips; sleep eyes; silk panties; rayon socks; drop earrings; pearl necklace; could also be ordered with hard plastic head and mohair wig; 1961.
One of the *Adorable Dress-Me Dolls*.

MARKS: None (doll)
SEE: *Illustration 197* (doll on right).
    Playthings, March 1961
PRICE: $5-10

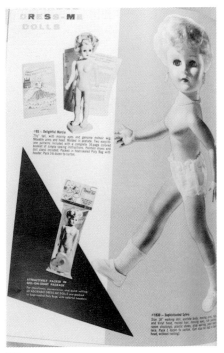

197.

Suzie: HP; 8in (20cm); toddler doll; mohair wig; jointed at neck, shoulders and arms; white shoes painted on over toes; (see *Illustration 428E*); sleep eyes; came with panties; one of the *Adorable Dress-Me Dolls*; circa 1959-1963; Dorothy Hesner of Chicago has such a doll and states, "Included was lots of printing which told how to dress the doll. Cottons and silks were the best. Use a curling iron to press the clothes. For fur trim use angora."

    MARKS: None (doll); "Adorable Dress Me Dolls//Sizes 7½ inch//to 20in (51cm) with moving eyes and moving parts//New Style Coiffeurs//Grant Plastics, Inc. Made in U.S.A." (cardboard attached to top of plastic bag)

    SEE: *Illustration 198. Playthings*, March 1961.

    PRICE: $5-10

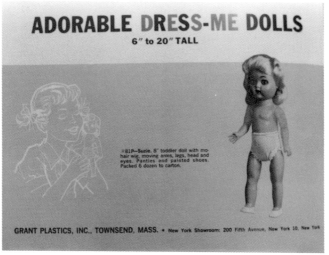

198.

Kathleen: HP; 11in (28cm); flat feet; sleep eyes; mohair wig; jointed at neck, shoulders and hips; individually packed in heat-sealed poly bag; doll stand included; one of the *Adorable Dress-Me Dolls*; circa 1959-1963.

    MARKS: None (doll)

    SEE: *Illustration 199* (doll on left). *Playthings*, March 1961.

    PRICE: $5-10

Priscilla: HP; 12in (31cm); high-heeled feet; mohair wig; jointed at neck, shoulders and hips; packed in heat-sealed poly bag; leotard and high-heeled shoes included; one of the *Adorable Dress-Me Dolls*; circa 1959-1963.

    MARKS: None (doll)

    SEE: *Illustration 199* (second from left). *Playthings*, March 1961.

    PRICE: $5-10

Linda: HP; 12in (31cm); teenage high-heeled feet; jointed at neck, shoulders and hips; mohair wig; high-heeled plastic shoes included; packed in heat-sealed poly bag; one of the *Adorable Dress-Me Dolls*; circa 1959-1963.

    MARKS: None (doll)

    SEE: *Illustration 199* (third from left). *Playthings*, March 1961.

    PRICE: $5-10

Gretchen: HP; 7½in (19cm); chubby baby doll-type; jointed at neck, shoulders and hips; sleep eyes; dynel wig; molded painted shoes (see *Illustration 198*); packed in heat sealed poly bag; circa 1959-1963.
   MARKS: None (doll)
   SEE: *Illustration 199* (fourth from left). *Playthings*, March 1961.
   PRICE: $5-10

Donna: HP; 7½in (19cm); sleep eyes; jointed at head and shoulders; mohair wig; stand included; painted shoes (see *Hard Plastic Dolls, I*, page 284D); one of the *Adorable Dress-Me Dolls*; circa 1959-1963.
   MARKS: None (doll)
   SEE: *Illustration 199* (fifth from left). *Playthings*, March 1961.
   PRICE: $5-10

Pamela: HP; 8in (20cm); sleep eyes; mohair wig; jointed at head and shoulders; high heeled; stand included; packed in heat resistant poly bag; one of the *Adorable Dress-Me Dolls*; circa 1959-1963.
   MARKS: None (doll)
   SEE: *Illustration 199* (sixth from left). *Playthings*, March 1961.
   PRICE: $5-10

Karen: HP; 7½in (19cm); sleep eyes; mohair wig; colorful removable plastic bra and panty set; painted shoes; packed in heat-sealed poly bag; stand included; one of the *Adorable Dress-Me Dolls*; circa 1959-1963.
   MARKS: None (doll)
   SEE: *Illustration 199* (seventh from left). *Playthings*, March 1961.
   PRICE: $5-10

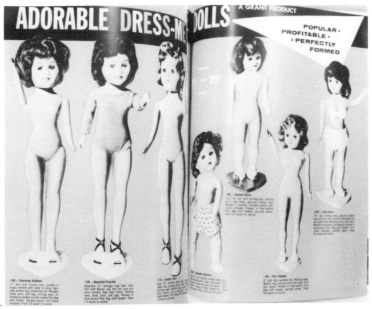

199.

Eileen: HP body with vinyl head; 20in (51cm); jointed at neck, shoulders, hips and knees; mohair wig; high-heeled feet; packed with earrings, necklace and bracelet; pearl tiara; 1960.

In 1959 they changed the finish on the faces of their dolls and advertised them as having "A New Sun-Tone." The dolls could be purchased dressed or undressed. *Eileen* was poly-packed in a box. It is one of the *Adorable Dress-Me Dolls.*

MARKS: None (doll)
SEE: *Illustration 200. Playthings,* March 1960.
PRICE: $10-12

200.

A reader, Elizabeth Woodward, of Leavenworth, Kansas, has reported that she has a doll like the "unknown" one on page 234, *Illustrations 519* and *520* in *Hard Plastic Dolls, I.* She said it was a "Dress-Me" doll. Grant made such a doll and sold it in a poly bag with a cardboard label. We are grateful to everyone who wrote to us through Hobby House Press, Inc., and many of the ideas and pictures in this book have come from these people. We enjoy each and every letter.

J. Halpern Company (Halco)

The registered trademarks, the trademarks and the copyrights appearing in italics within this chapter belong to J. Halpern Company.

In the early 1950s the J. Halpern Company advertised rather large "Pretty as a Picture" dolls. They advertised in *Playthings* in 1951 but no further advertisements for the company could be found. Upper left: doll in checked long dress with umbrella and purse. Middle right: *Baby Fluffee*. Lower left: doll in formal dress with white stole. In 1951 their 12-page catalog featured these and many other dolls.

> **SEE:** *Illustration 201. Playthings,* April 1951.

Baby Fluffee: HP head with magic skin body; 24in (61cm); flirty blue sleep eyes; blonde mohair wig; off-white dress with pink ribbons; the same embroidery design is on bonnet and skirt of dress; rubber panties which have a tendency to melt onto magic skin body; circa 1951.

> **MARKS:** None (doll); navy blue tag with gold writing, "Superb//Halco//Brand//Made in U.S.A.//Baby Fluffee//featherweight"
>
> **SEE:** *Illustration 202. Sandy Strater Collection.*
>
> **PRICE:** $50-65

201.

202.

Bride doll: HP; 29in (74cm); gown of lustrous white rayon satin; illusion veil; white slippers; 1951.

Bridesmaid: HP; 29in (74cm); flowered dress with ruffle around bottom of skirt; 1951.

> SEE: *Illustration 203. Playthings,* June 1951.
> PRICE: $85-110

203.

Hardy Different Toys

The registered trademarks, the trademarks and the copyrights appearing in italics within this chapter belong to Hardy Different Toys.

Girl in White Dress: HP; 14in (36cm); light brown mohair wig; blue sleep eyes; white satin and net trimmed with gold rickrack costume; 1949. The owner was given this doll for a Christmas present in 1949. It had been purchased at Schrafft's in New York City.

> MARKS: "Made in USA" (back); "Hardy Different Toys// Trade Mark//New York, N.Y. 23 E. 49th St." (on diamond shaped tag)
> SEE: *Illustration 204. Mary Elizabeth Poole Collection.*
> PRICE: $75-100

204.

P. J. Hill Co.

The registered trademarks, the trademarks and the copyrights appearing in italics within this chapter belong to P. J. Hill, Co., unless otherwise noted.

Based in Newark, New Jersey, this is another marketing company which sold by mail order. They purchased dolls from known companies and advertised them heavily in the hobby and "pulp" magazines of the 1950s. Today we would say that they "discounted" them. The dolls sold widely and well, and today they are very collectible. Most of them are unmarked.

Cindy Walker: HP; 14in (36cm), 20in (51cm) and 23in (58cm); braided hair; sleep eyes; head-turning walker; jointed at neck, shoulders and hips; mama voice; *Saucy Walker* look-alike; extra wardrobe could be ordered including hat and coat ensemble, bridal ensemble, plaid vinyl rain cape, ballerina outfit, hostess coat and sheer nightgown; 1955.

SEE: *Illustration 205. Workbasket,* November 1955.

PRICE: $25-35

205.

Saucy Walker® is a registered trademark of the Ideal Toy Corporation.

Hollywood Doll Manufacturing Co.

The registered trademarks, the trademarks and the copyrights appearing in italics within this chapter belong to Hollywood Doll Manufacturing Co., unless otherwise noted.

Queen for a Day: HP; 6in (15cm); painted eyes looking upward; molded hair under wig; swivel head; protruding lower stomach; 1st, 2nd, 3rd and 4th fingers molded together; red velvet robe with mock fur trim; white satin and lace dress; gold crown; 1947. The doll was made for the popular program "Queen for a Day." It was advertised in *Playthings*, March 1947.
   MARKS: Star "Hollywood Dolls" (back)
   SEE: *Illustration 206.*
   PRICE: $28-30

Western Series Cowboy: HP; 5in (13cm); sleep eyes; no eyelashes; molded hair; all fingers molded together; original clothes; black cowboy hat; red checked shirt; imitation brown leather pants; black painted-on shoes; circa 1947.
   MARKS: "Hollywood Dolls" in circle (back); wrist tag says "Cowboy;" box labeled "A Hollywood Doll//Western Series//Cowboy."
   SEE: *Illustration 207.*
   PRICE: $20-30

206.

207.

Advertisement in *Playthings*, September 1952: list of dolls and other items available in 1951.

Princess Series
Lucky Star Series
Nursery Rhymes
Little Friends
Playmates
Toyland Series
Sweetheart Series
Lullaby Baby Series
Western Series

Everyday Series
Cradle Series
Baby Buggy Series
The Lucky Star Doll
Queen for a Day
The Wishing Doll
Old Mother Witch
The Nun
Peter Rabbit

Bunny Rabbit
Bridegroom
Ballerina
Undressed
Bedtime Dolly
Little Snow Baby
Doll Stands
Cradle
Carriage

SEE: *Illustration 208.*

208.

Non-walking doll: HP; 8in (20cm); unusual shiny brown wig; non-walking doll; unusual brown sleep eyes; molded eyelashes; no painted lashes; jointed at neck, shoulders and hips; straighter legs than most of the small *Ginny*®-type dolls; individual fingers; arms have unusual indentations at the elbows; arms and legs are not strung like similar dolls but move well; feet have dimples above toes; only slight indentation for navel; mid 1950s; (see Identification Section, *Illustration 415.*)

  MARKS: Large Star with "A Hollywood Doll" around outer edge (back)
  SEE: *Illustration 209. Marge Meisinger Collection.*
  PRICE: $25-35

209.

Ginny® is a registered trademark of the Vogue Dolls, Inc.

Rock-a-Bye Baby: HP; 5in (13cm); jointed neck and arms; all original in box; white taffeta with lace and ribbon trim; circa 1949-1951.

    MARKS: "Hollywood Doll" in circle (back); "Hollywood Doll" (arm tag); "Rock-a-by-Baby" (box)

    SEE: *Illustration 210. Pat Parton Collection.*

    PRICE: $16-20

210.

Horsman Dolls, Inc.

The registered trademarks, the trademarks and the copyrights appearing in italics within this chapter belong to Horsman Dolls, Inc.

Pitter Patty: HP head; soft body; vinyl arms and legs; 19in (48cm); sleep eyes; crier; heart beat mechanism without winding; plastic curlers for curling her hair.

    SEE: *Illustration 211. Playthings,* November 1951.

    PRICE: $50-65

211.

124

Mary Had a Little Lamb: HP; 18in (46cm); excellent color; blonde mohair wig; black eye shadow; orange feathered eyelashes; Y on backside; all original (possibly dressed by Mollye Goldman); pink embossed organdy dress; white organdy apron; white pantaloons; circa 1953-1955.

    MARKS: "Horsman" (head)
    SEE: *Illustration 212. Ester Borgis Collection.*
    PRICE: $85-110

Little Girl: HP; 16in (41cm); excellent color; sleep eyes; open mouth with four teeth; felt tongue; individual fingers; original clothes; pink taffeta dress with plaid taffeta trim; early 1950s.

    MARKS: "Horsman" (head); "This Horsman doll has Saran hair, sleep eyes; real lashes." (tag)
    SEE: *Illustration 213. Gigi Williams Collection.*
    PRICE: $70-90

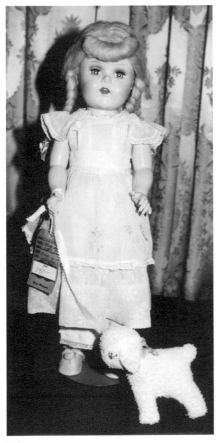

212.

213.

Bright Star: HP; 15in (38cm); sleep eyes; open mouth with teeth; original clothes; head turning walker; pretty ponytail; blue piqué dress with white collar and cuffs; red and white braid only on one collar and down the front; Saran hair; blue plastic shoes; early 1950s.

MARKS: None (doll); "Bright Star// Horsman//All Plastic// Lightweight and Non- Breakable//Lifelike and Washable//Arms, Legs, Head Moves" (tag)

SEE: *Illustration 214. Chree Kysar Collection.*

PRICE: $70-90

214.

Mary Hoyer Doll Mfg. Co.

The registered trademarks, the trademarks and the copyrights appearing in italics within this chapter belong to Mary Hoyer Doll Mfg. Co.

Bride: HP; 14in (36cm); glass-like sleep eyes; closed mouth; 2nd and 3rd fingers slightly curled; pointed chin; tiny face in comparison with other hard plastic dolls; beautiful porcelain-like skin color; standard arms (see Identification Guide, *Hard Plastic Dolls, I*, page 262A); real lashes and lashes painted under eyes; eye shadow; jointed in neck, arms and legs; no molded hair under wig; gray eyebrows; original satin dress with net overskirt; bodice with net ruffle; matching veil; late 1940s to mid 1950s.

MARKS: "Original//Mary Hoyer//Doll" in circle (back); "Mary//Hoyer//Dolls" (box)

SEE: *Illustration 215* (Color Section, page 168). *Pat Parton Collection.*

PRICE: $350-400 + depending on costume; prices vary in different sections of the country.

Mary Hoyer Dollies: (for general characteristics, see *Illustration 215*). From left to right: girl in handknit beige dress; Mary Hoyer labeled nurse's outfit with blue cape and hat with a red cross of felt; gray skirt and Mary Hoyer labeled burgundy sweater set; dark green short coat and hat set; beige and white tennis outfit with tennis racket; late 1940s to mid 1950s.

MARKS: "Original//Mary//Hoyer//Doll" in circle (back)

SEE: *Illustration 216. Sharlene Doyle Collection.*

PRICE: $350-400+ depending on costume; prices vary in different sections of the country

216.

217.

Doll in Three-Piece Knitted Bathing Outfit: HP; 14in (36cm); (for general characteristics, see *Illustration 215*). Mary Hoyer sold dolls and doll patterns through a mail order business in Reading, Pennsylvania. This doll wears a deep pink three-piece bathing suit knitted from an original pattern.

MARKS: "Original//Mary Hoyer// Doll" in circle (back).

SEE: *Illustration 217.*

PRICE: $350-400+ depending on costume; prices vary in different sections of the country

127

Molded Hair *Mary Hoyer:* HP; 14in
(36cm); (for general characteristics, see *Illustration 215*). It is not unusual for a Mary
Hoyer doll to have slightly molded hair
under the original wig. This doll has a dark
brown wig over the molded hair.

MARKS: "Original//Mary Hoyer//
Doll" in circle (back)

SEE: *Illustration 218. Helen Keefe Collection.*

Walking Doll in *Polly Prim* Outfit: HP;
14in (36cm); (for general characteristics
see, *Illustration 215*); for $.75 plus the reg-
ular price of $4.95, a walking doll could be
ordered; doll came with Dupont nylon
washable wig; the same doll with a hand-
curled wig was $3.50; other items which
could be ordered included a sewing kit to
make a *Polly Prim* outfit; a ready-to-wear
Polly Prim outfit; yarn kits and accessories;
Dolly Wave set; wardrobe trunks; *Sun
Bonnet Sue* Child's Sewing Kit; and *Sun
Bonnet Sue* outfit ready to wear.

SEE: *Illustration 219. McCall's Needlework*, Fall-Winter 1953-1954.

219.

218.

128

Twins: HP; 14in (36cm); boy (see *Hard Plastic Dolls, I,* page 112) and girl; (for general characteristics, see *Illustration 215*); 1953. The advertisement said, "You and your little girl will find real enjoyment in these famous twin dolls." The girl has a Dupont nylon washable wig that can be combed or waved. The boy's hair is of curly lamb's wool dyed brown or black. Both came undressed but with shoes and stockings.

    MARKS: "Original//Mary Hoyer//Doll" in circle (back)

    SEE: *Illustration 220. McCall's Needlework,* Spring-Summer 1953.

Mary Hoyer: HP; 14in (36cm); advertisement for yarn kits and accessories; kit to make Western Costume was $1.00; western boots were $.35; kits included all necessary materials, buttons, simple instructions; sports accessories available included roller skates, ice skates, skis and tennis rackets.

    SEE: *Illustration 221. McCall's Needlework,* Winter 1949-50.

220.

221.

Gigi: HP; 18in (46cm); sleep eyes; only about 2000 of these dolls were made by the Frisch Doll Company; pink long satin dress; pink straw hat; early 1950s.

MARKS: "Original//Mary Hoyer//Doll" in circle (back)

SEE: *Illustration 222. Kathy George Collection.*

PRICE: $400-500+ (very few sample prices available)

222.

Ideal Toy Corporation

The registered trademarks, the trademarks and the copyrights appearing in italics within this chapter belong to Ideal Toy Corporation, unless otherwise noted.

The Ideal Toy and Novelty Company was one of the doll industry's leaders during the hard plastic era. Today's collectors have realized that their *Toni®*, *Saucy Walker* and *Miss Curity* dolls are very beautiful and very collectible. Prices have risen accordingly.

The authors were happy to have presented the company catalogs in *Hard Plastic Dolls, I* and in this book they have attempted to show the unusual and rarer dolls in the Ideal line.

Many readers have asked us for more information about the wonderful Ideal babies. We have featured some of them in this volume. Perhaps the doll we have been asked to identify most often is the all-hard plastic *Plassie Toddler* which is one of the most beautiful of all the hard plastic babies. (See *Illustrations 224-226*).

Just before the company went out of business we asked the Ideal Public Relations Department to try to find out if there were unmarked Ideal dolls. They contacted foremen on the line who had been there in the 1950s, and they said that some of the regular lines were unmarked and purchased for special orders. They particularly made the *Toni*-type dolls in formal dresses for special orders.

Because many of their customers wanted the new vinyl heads with rooted hair, they substituted these vinyl heads for hard plastic heads or hard plastic heads for vinyl heads as they had requests. They sold regular dolls to the leading mail order houses and also made special dolls for them, both marked and unmarked.

For detailed information about Ideal dolls, see *Hard Plastic Dolls, I*, pages 122-163.

Plassie: HP head with pliable synthetic rubber body; 16in (41cm), 19in (48cm) and 22in (60cm); cries when leg is squeezed; sleep eyes with real lashes; separate fingers; fingers so flexible that doll can clasp her hands; cotton-stuffed body; dress of embroidered sheer pastel cotton; matching bonnet; cotton slip; panties; rayon socks; imitation leather shoes; 1946. This is a very early doll with a hard plastic head and a magic skin body.

SEE: *Illustration 223*. Sears catalog, Christmas 1946. *Barbara Andresen Collection.*

PRICE: $50-100 (depending on size and costume)

223.

Toni® is a registered trademark of The Gillette Co.

131

Plassie Toddler: both dolls are all-HP; 14in (36cm).

Most of the Ideal babies and toddlers during this period had a hard plastic head and a "Magic Skin" or cloth body, but the *Plassie Toddler* was listed in the 1949-1950 catalog as having "a new all plastic body, sleeping eyes, fully jointed, mohair wig." (See *Hard Plastic Dolls, I,* page 131.) Ideal did offer changes in doll specifications and parts in this catalog. Probably some doll buyers wanted to offer their customers the molded hair dolls which mothers often preferred instead of wigs which could be pulled off easily by children.

Both dolls are similar but they have different characteristics. Doll on left: blue sleep eyes; painted lashes under the eyes; closed mouth; painted brown hair.

MARKS: "Made in U.S.A.//Pat. No. 2252077" (head); "Ideal Doll//14" (back)

Doll on right: hazel sleep eyes; eyebrows; lashes painted under eyes; painted brown hair; molded curls on back of head; open mouth; pink blush on cheeks, elbows and chest; original shoes and socks.

MARKS: "14//Ideal Doll//Made in U.S.A." (head); "Ideal Doll//14" (back); "An Ultra Fine Product//An//Ideal Doll//Made in USA//Ideal Novelty & Toy Co.//Long Island City//New York" (tag)

SEE: *Illustration 224* (front). *Elaine Timm Collection.*
Illustration 225 (back). *Elaine Timm Collection.*

PRICE: $75-100

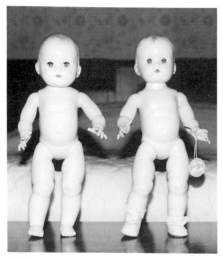

224. 225.

Plassie Toddler: HP; 14in (36cm); sleep eyes; jointed at neck and shoulders; dark wig with curls; dressed in yellow organdy dress and bonnet with the unique Ideal trim around the bottom of the dress; circa 1949-1950. This doll was in the 1949-1950 catalog (see *Hard Plastic Dolls, I,* page 131, *Illustration 310).*

MARKS: "14//Ideal Doll//Made in U.S.A." (head); "Ideal Doll//14" (body)

SEE: *Illustration 226. Ruth Moss Collection.*

PRICE: $75-100

226.

227.

228.

Betsy Wetsy: HP head; synthetic rubber body; 12in (31cm) and 16in (41cm); sleeping eyes with real lashes; six-piece layette and nursing bottle; dressed in knitted shirt, flannel diapers, knitted bootees; layette includes cotton print frock and bonnet, rayon socks, imitation leather shoes; 1946.

SEE: *Illustration 227.* Sears catalog, Christmas 1946. *Barbara Andresen Collection.*

PRICE: $80-100

Which Doll is the *Toni*: advertisement for the *Toni* doll which was a "take-off" on the famous commerical of the time, "Which twin has the Toni Home Permanent?"

SEE: *Illustration 228. Family Circle,* December 1950.

Toni* Family Common Characteristics: HP; closed mouth; sleep eyes with lashes; painted lashes below eyes; individual fingers with four dimples on back of hand; two dimples behind the knee; standard arm (see Identification Guide, *Hard Plastic Dolls, I,* page 262A); line around wrist; usually well marked; pretty flesh tone; Y on seat; washable and curlable hair.

MARKS:		PRICE:	
"Ideal Doll"			P 90 $150-180
"P 90"	14in (36cm)		P 91 $160-190
"P 91"	16in (41cm)		P 92 $190-250
"P 92"	19in (48cm)		P 93 $275-330
"P 93"	21in (53cm)		P 94 $350-400+ (very few
"P 94"	22½in (57cm)		sample prices available)

Toni,* Ideal's Nylon Haired, Nylon-Dressed Beauty: HP; introduction of Bur-Mil nylon permanent pleated dress for *Toni** doll; 1953.
SEE: *Illustration 229. Playthings,* March 1953.

Toni* in Pleated Dress: HP; 21in (53cm); (for general characteristics, see above); medium blue nylon accordian-pleated dress; pink leather shoes; rose ribbon sash; rose wrist ties on arms; blue satin ribbon in hair; petticoat not attached to dress; lace on dress, petticoat and panties is the same.
MARKS: "P-93" (neck and back)
SEE: *Illustration 230. Jean Dicus Collection.*
PRICE: $400 up (rare doll; very few sample prices)

229.

230.

Toniˑ: HP; 16in (41cm); blonde wig; all original tagged dress; pink top and blue and gold skirt; excellent skin coloring; came with *Toni Wave Kit; circa 1952.*
  MARKS: "Ideal Doll P 91" (head)
  SEE: *Illustration 231* (Color Section, page 166).
  PRICE: $160-180

Toni **Patterns:** HP; (for general characteristics, see page 134). Many patterns were available "at your favorite pattern counter." The advertising stated the patterns could also be worn by "famous Ideal's other 'Dolls with a Purpose:' Harriet Hubbard Ayer, Betsy McCall and Miss Curity."
  SEE: *Illustration 232. McCall's Needlework,* Fall-Winter 1953-1954.

232.

233.

Harriet Hubbard Ayer: HP body and vinyl head; came in 14in (36cm), 16in (41cm), 19in (48cm) and 21in (53cm); introduced at New York Toy Fair in February 1953; came with eight-piece harmless *Harriet Hubbard Ayer* cosmetic kit, beauty table and booklet of instructions; 1953.

MARKS: "MK 14 Ideal Doll" (head); "Ideal Doll" (back)

SEE: *Illustration 233. Playthings,* March 1953.

PRICE: $140-180 14in (36cm)
$175-200 16in (41cm)

Miss Curity: HP; 14in (36cm); (for general characteristics, see page 134); unusual picture of dark-haired *Miss Curity;* made only in 14in (36cm) size; included with the doll was a complete Bauer & Black first aid kit; box included a booklet of first aid play instructions; 1953.

MARKS: "P 90//Ideal Doll//Made in USA" (head); "Ideal Doll//P 90" (back)

SEE: *Illustration 234. Playthings,* March 1953.

PRICE: $200-225

234.

Mary Hartline (Toni• P-94): HP; 22½in (57cm); closed mouth; sleep eyes with lashes; painted lashes below eyes; individual fingers with four dimples on back of hand; two dimples behind the knee; line around wrist; usually well marked; pretty flesh tone; Y̌ on seat; washable and curlable hair; grill in stomach; 1952.

> MARKS: "Ideal" (head); "P 94" (body); "P 93" (arms)
> SEE: *Illustration 235. Patricia Arches Collection.*
> PRICE: $300-350 up (rare doll)

Toni•: HP; 22½in (57cm); unusually large *Toni•* doll; all original; red dress with rickrack trim around neckline; gold belt and shoes; excellent skin coloring; black wig; sleep eyes; (for general *Toni•* P 94 characteristics, see *Illustration 325*).

> MARKS: "P 94" (back of head)
> SEE: *Illustration 236. Chree Kysar Collection.*
> PRICE: $300-350 up (rare doll)

Betsy McCall® (Toni• family): vinyl head with wig; HP body; 14in (36cm); closed mouth; sleep eyes and lashes; wears real *Betsy McCall®* clothes just like the dresses little girls shopped for at department stores; fully-jointed; an easy-to-sew pattern came with every *Betsy McCall®*; there were also paper dolls of *Betsy* each month in *McCall's®* magazine; all original outfit; rose skirt with straps and white blouse; 1953.

> MARKS: "McCall Corp." (head); "P 90//Ideal Doll" (back)
> SEE: *Illustration 237* (Color Section, page 169).
> PRICE: $150-170

235.

236.

Saucy Walker: HP; 22in (56cm); jointed head turning walker; flirty rolling eyes; Saran wig which could be brushed and waved; grill in stomach (see Identification Guide, *Hard Plastic Dolls, I,* page 276D); open mouth with two teeth; individual fingers; painted eyelashes under eyes; pin-jointed walker with unpainted Ideal screw type pin (see Identification Guide, *Hard Plastic Dolls, I,* page 290B); straight legs; red dot in corner of eye; double crease behind knee; circa 1952.

MARKS: "Ideal" (head)
SEE: *Illustration 238. Sharlene Doyle Collection.*
PRICE: $125-150 22in (56cm)
$70-100 16in (41cm)

Lolly: HP; 9in (23cm); walker with turning head; pin-jointed walker; pin covered with paint; two dimples on knees; painted-molded hair with curls covering ear; individual fingers; closed mouth; molded lashes; not original clothes; circa early 1950s. This is the doll listed as *Tiny Girl* on page 143 of *Hard Plastic Dolls, I.* Elizabeth Woodward of Leavenworth, Kansas, wrote to tell us her name. Kathryn Davis of Toledo, Ohio, supplied the Ideal brochure. We thank them both.

SEE: *Illustration 239. Ideal Brochure.*
PRICE: $25-30

238.

239.

Inez Holland House

Starlet: HP; 7½in (19cm); wardrobe consists of school dresses, "Sunday best," sportswear, bridal party and special costumes; costumes were stain resistant and wiped clean with a damp cloth; circa 1957.
Inez Holland House was a company which sold many types of dolls made by other manufacturers.
   MARKS: None (doll)
   SEE: *Illustration 192.* Luster-Creme Shampoo Starlet Brochure.
   PRICE: $30-35

192.

Jolly Toys

Girl in Pink Dress: HP; 16in (41cm); sleep eyes; beautiful blonde wig; open mouth with two teeth; jointed at neck, shoulders and hips; all original; pink taffeta dress with lace trim; rose at waistline; snap slippers; circa 1954-55.
   MARKS: None (doll); "Jolly Toys" (tag)
   SEE: *Illustration 240. Ester Borgis Collection.*
   PRICE: $60-75

240.

Joy Toys, Inc.

The registered trademarks, the trademarks and the copyrights appearing in italics within this chapter belong to Joy Toys, Inc.

Talking Doll: Speaks in English, Spanish, French or Portuguese; company advertised that they made rubber dolls, composition dolls, talking dolls and plastic dolls; 1951. SEE: *Illustration 241. Playthings*, May 1951.

241.

Kim Dolls

The registered trademarks, the trademarks and the copyrights appearing in italics within this chapter belong to Kim Dolls.

Fairy: HP; 8½in (22cm); (for general characteristics, see Virga *Hi Heel 'Teen, Illustrations 368, 369*). This is an example of several satellite marketing companies operating from one main company. Both boxes had the same address (47 West St., New York City). Both dolls had wardrobes designed for the individual doll. However, the costumes fit both dolls. Circa 1956-1957.

MARKS: None (doll); "Kim//Ready to Dress" (box)

SEE: *Illustration 242. Marge Meisinger Collection.*

PRICE: $20-25

242.

Kim in Jodhpur Outfit: HP with vinyl head; 7½in (19cm); (for general characteristics, see Fortune-Virga dolls, page 112); original costume; circa 1956-1957. This doll wears the same costume as the Virga doll in *Illustration 364*. Both dolls were made by the Beehler Arts Company and distributed under different names.

MARKS: None (doll); "Kim//Riding Outfit" (box)

SEE: *Illustration 243. Patricia Arches Collection.*

PRICE: $20-25

243.

Käthe Kruse

The registered trademarks, the trademarks and the copyrights appearing in italics within this chapter belong to Käthe Kruse.

Because cloth dolls had become very expensive for Käthe Kruse to manufacture in the 1950s, she turned to the German Schildkröte celluloid firm for help in making a new doll made entirely of a mixture of celluloid and plastic. This has now come to be called hard plastic. However, it is not quite the same material as the hard plastic made in the United States during this period.

A few years later production on these dolls ceased and a new doll was designed and produced which had a type of hard plastic head and a cloth body.

Model Hanne Kruse: European HP head; 9¾in (25cm); cloth body; German-style dress with white apron; all original; circa 1957.

MARKS: "Original//Käthe Kruse// Model//Hanne Kruse" (tag); "G.M.6.H. 885" (label in dress)

SEE: *Illustration 244. Beatrice Campbell Collection.*

PRICE: $250-275 up

244.

Badebaby: HP; approximately 12in (31cm); head was that of "Rumpumpel" doll; body made by Rheinische Gummi und Celluloid Fabrik Co. (turtle symbol); entirely washable; 1963-1974.

    MARKS: None (doll)

    SEE: *Illustration 245. Mary Elizabeth Poole Collection.*

    PRICE: $300-350 up (very few sample prices available)

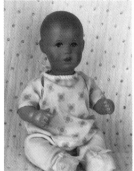

245.

#5934/10 Gretchen (left) and #5964/1 Hansel (right): all-HP; 16in (41cm); unusual sleep eyes (the lid comes down and the whole ball of the eye does not roll); wigs; *Gretchen* is dressed in the traditional German jumper; *Hansel* is dressed in Bavarian-type short pants with suspenders of braid; circa mid 1950s.

    MARKS: Turtle in Diamond//"Modell//Käthe Kruse//T46"

    SEE: *Illustration 246. Mary Elizabeth Poole Collection.*

    PRICE: $375-400 up each

#5934/11 Susi (left) and **#5954/6 Jane** (right): all-HP; 16in (41cm); unusual sleep eyes (the lid comes down and the whole ball of eye does not roll); wigs; dressed in traditional jumpers of the young German schoolgirl; mid 1950s.

    MARKS: Turtle in Diamond//"Modell//Käthe Kruse//T46" (head)

    SEE: *Illustration 247. Mary Elizabeth Poole Collection.*

    PRICE: $375-400 each

246.

247.

Mimerle: German HP head; cloth body; approximately 12in (31cm); polka dot dress with white apron; human hair pigtail wig; painted eyes; purchased in 1972. The quality of the hard plastic head on this doll is not quite the same as that on the earlier all-HP dolls.

MARKS: "Original//Käthe Kruse// Stoffpuppe" (tag)

SEE *Illustration 248. Mary Elizabeth Poole Collection.*

PRICE: $300-400 up

248.

Mrs. Lavalle

The registered trademarks, the trademarks and the copyrights appearing in italics within this chapter belong to Mrs. Lavalle.

249.

Cuddlee Bride Walking Doll: HP; 8in (20cm); jointed at neck, shoulders and hips; sleep eyes; came complete with seven outfits; price complete in 1956, $2.98. This is another of the popular small walking dolls which was marketed by a special company. In this case it was a mail order company. It is impossible from the advertisement to identify the doll.

SEE: *Illustration 249. House Beautiful,* October 1956. *Margaret Mandel Collection.*

PRICE: $25-30

Lenci (Italy)

The Lenci company is known for their cloth dolls of the 1920s and 1930s. However, the well-known Italian company has been making many different kinds of dolls and novelties throughout their existence.

After World War II they used the new hard plastic for several different lines of dolls. They had been making the cloth *Miniatures* and *Mascotte* dolls dressed in provincial costumes, and they continued to make provincial dolls in the new plastic material. These dolls are dressed in the usual quality costumes of the House of Lenci.
From left to right:

Girl from Sardinia: HP; 6in (15cm); beautiful hand-painted face with the Lenci two-tone lips; side glancing eyes; tiny hand-painted eyelashes; fingers molded together; light brown wig; red felt skirt and bolero with metallic trim; black apron with embroidered waistband; white cotton print scarf under her brown felt headdress; 1950s.

    MARKS: "Lenci//Torino//Made in Italy//Samughed//Sardegna" (tag)
    SEE: *Illustration 250* (Color Section, page 223).
    PRICE: $40-50

Girl from Valsarentino: HP with vinyl arms; 6in (15cm); lovely flesh tone to the hard plastic; well-painted face with the usual Lenci two-tone lips; side-glancing eyes with tiny painted eyelashes; blue eye shadow above eyes; red felt skirt and top; blue and red plaid scarf; white print apron; gold necklace with "Torino" engraved on it; black felt provincial hat with blue and white ribbons; 1950s.

    MARKS: "Lenci//Torino" (tag sewn into seam of dress)
    SEE: *Illustration 250* (Color Section, page 223).
    PRICE: $40-50

Lovely Doll

251.

U.S. Marine, U.S. Army, U.S. Air Corps: HP; 7in (18cm); fluttery eyes; high arched eyebrows; lashes painted above eyes; one-piece body; arm and neck joints, 2nd and 3rd fingers molded together; painted-on shoes with bows (see *Hard Plastic Dolls, I*, Identification Guide, page 286J); standard arm hook; two marks on palms of hands; molded painted hair; dressed in traditional uniforms; circa 1954.

    MARKS: None (doll); "A Lovely Doll//Movable eyes, Movable arms, Movable head" (box)
    SEE: *Illustration 251.*
    PRICE: $15-18 each

McCall's Patterns and Kits

The registered trademarks, the trademarks and the copyrights appearing in italics within this chapter belong to McCall's, unless otherwise noted.

Pattern for Dy-Dee® Doll: patterns for a lacy party dress: embroidered Sunday coat; sunsuit; bunting; came in sizes for 11in (28cm), 13in (33cm), 15in (38cm) and 20in (51cm) dolls.

SEE: *Illustration 252. McCall's Needlework*, Winter 1949-1950.

XMAS FOR DOLLY

Dress a Dy-Dee Doll in the Xmas spirit. She'll wear a lacy party dress under her embroidered Sunday coat. Cute sunsuit outfit. A bunting for sleepy-time. For dolls 11, 13, 15, 20 ins. No. 632, blue transfer, 25c.

252.

No. 1720. Bicycling outfit for a Sweet Sue doll—pedal pushers, jersey blouse and kerchief. Also, three other outfits. For dolls 15, 18, 21 inches tall. Pattern, electric blue transfer, 35c.

No. 1706. Sunsuit for a Toni doll—back, front and sleeves cut in one piece, zippered closing. Also, three other outfits. EASILY MADE. For dolls 14, 16, 19, 21 inches tall. Pattern, 35c.

No. 1809. Appliquéd felt skirt for Maggie and Alice dolls. Petti-blouse, knitted sweater and cap, party dress. Also, other clothes. For 15, 18 in. dolls. Pattern, McCall's Blue* transfer, 35c.

*"McCall's Blue" transfer stamps on light or dark material

253.

Patterns for Dolls: HP dolls; various sizes depending on dolls; patterns for pedal pushers with jersey blouse and kerchief for *Sweet Sue®* dolls; sunsuit for *Toni®* dolls; appliqued felt skirt for *Maggie®* and *Alice®* dolls; party dress for *Maggie®* and *Alice®* dolls; 1953-1954.

SEE: *Illustration 253. McCall's Needlework*, Fall-Winter 1953-1954.

Sweet Sue® is a registered trademark of the American Character Doll Co.
Toni® is a registered trademark of The Gillette Co.
Alice® is a registered trademark of the Alexander Doll Co.
Maggie® is a registered trademark of the Alexander Doll Co.

Betsy McCall: HP; 14in (36cm); pictures of costumes from some of the McCall patterns available at local stores; advertised as "easily made, close with zippers."
SEE: *Illustration 254. McCalls Needlework*, Fall-Winter 1953-1954.

254.

Doll Kits for Majorette Cowgirl and Skater: HP walking dolls; complete kit included doll, wool yarn, accessories and instructions.
SEE: *Illustration 255. McCall's Needlework*, Fall-Winter 1953-1954.
      Illustration 256. McCall's Needlework, Fall-Winter 1953-1954.

255. M<small>C</small>CALL'S   256.

Fad of the Month Club Doll: offer to readers of *McCall's Needlework*; you could select a sewing kit to dress the club doll as a *Bride, Angel* or *Sweet Genevive*; each month there was another offering; dolls were all-HP.

SEE: *Illustration 257. McCall's Needlework,* Fall-Winter 1953-1954.

257.

McCall's Needlework Magazine (D.M.C. Corp.)

Famous Women in History Crochet Costume Instructions Book: for HP "Dress Me" type dolls. Costumes include:

1. Top left - *Marie Antoinette*
2. Top right - *Queen Elizabeth*
3. Center left - *Joan of Arc*
4. Center right - *Cleopatra*
5. Bottom left to right - *Queen Ester, Queen Isabella, Betsy Ross, Empress Josephine* and *Mary, Queen of Scots.*

SEE: *Illustration 258. McCall's Needlework,* Fall-Winter 1953-54.

Marie Antoinette®, Queen Elizabeth®, Joan of Arc®, Cleopatra®, Queen Ester®, Queen Isabella®, Betsy Ross®, Empress Josephine® and *Mary, Queen of Scots®* are registered trademarks of D.M.C. Corp.

258.

Romeo and Juliet: HP; 32in (81cm); mannequins which were used by the sewing classes of Bedford High School (suburban Cleveland, Ohio) for a project in costume design: *Juliet* is dressed in pink velvet and lace with a chiffon scarf; *Romeo* wears a dark blue tunic with a medium blue cape; circa 1950s.

MARKS: "McCall" (base of doll)
SEE: *Illustration 259. Thelma Purvis Collection.*
PRICE: No price samples available.

259.

Midwestern Mfg. Co.

The registered trademarks, the trademarks and the copyrights appearing in italics within this chapter belong to Midwestern Mfg. Co, unless otherwise noted.

Mary Jean: HP; 8in (20cm); blonde hair; large eyes; jointed at neck, shoulders and hips; arm hook (see Identification Guide, page 236E); dress has blue top with blue, black and yellow print skirt; gold ribbon sash; walking mechanism, head does not turn; separate fingers; white shoes painted over bare feet so toes show through; (see Identification Guide, page 251E); all original clothes; excellent skin color; doll has most *Ginger®* characteristics but the hard plastic is inferior; arm hooks (see Identification Guide, page 238); circa 1954-1956.

MARKS: None (body); "I'm Mary Jean//A Product of Midwestern Manufacturing Co." (box)
SEE: *Illustration 260.*
PRICE: $23-26

Ginger® is a registered trademark of Cosmopolitan Toy and Doll Corporation.

260.
150

261.

Suzy Stroller: HP; 16in (41cm) and 19in (48cm); walker; 1953.

Midwestern Mfg. Co. made a line of inexpensive dolls for the mass market. In the same magazine they advertised "America's Famous Character Dolls", 6½in (17cm), 7½in (19cm) and 11in (28cm).

MARKS: Most bodies of Midwestern dolls are unmarked but the boxes usually have the Midwestern name on them.

SEE: *Illustration 261. Playthings,* March 1953.

PRICE: $50-75

Nancy Ann Storybook Dolls, Inc.

The registered trademarks, the trademarks and the copyrights appearing in italics within this chapter belong to Nancy Ann Storybook Dolls, Inc., unless otherwise noted.

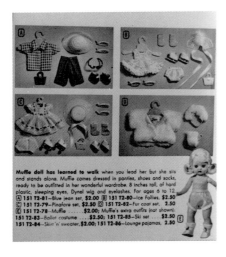

Muffie **Identification:** *Muffie* was introduced in 1953 to compete with the small dolls such as *Ginny*₅. They were introduced as "Playtime Dolls." They came both dressed and undressed in a basic box. Nancy Ann produced an extensive wardrobe for these tiny 8in (20cm) dolls, constantly changing the line to compete with the many other small dolls which flooded the market.

Nine basic types of dolls are shown in the Identification Section, pages 240, 241. All are similar except #9 which was made after the original company was sold.

Muffie: HP; 8in (20cm); jointed on head, arms and legs only; Dynel wigs and eyelashes; sleep eyes; pictured is a blue jean set, pinafore set, Ice Follies costume, fur coat set; 1954. According to the advertisement, this was the year that *Muffie* learned to walk.

SEE: *Illustration 262.* Marshall Field & Co. 1954 Christmas catalog. *Barbara Andresen Collection.*

PRICE: $85-100+ (according to costume)

263.

Nancy Ann *Muffie* Brochure: (top to bottom)
Left to right: Row 1

    501 White dress with red trim and hair ribbon.
    502 Pink dress with blue trim and hair ribbon.
    503 Dress with red skirt and red and white polka dot top.
    504 Dress with rose top; white print skirt; rose hair ribbon.
    505 Dress with blue top with rickrack trim; yellow skirt with blue print.
    506 Dress with blue top trimmed with lace; pink print skirt.
    507 Blue and white striped dress trimmed in red; red hair ribbon.
    508 Pink dress trimmed with blue; large blue hair ribbon.

Left to right: Row 2
  601 Lavender and white striped dress; white tam.
  602 Yellow dress with deeper yellow trim; straw hat with one daisy.
  603 Blue print dress with pattern of white stripes with blue polka dots; red cloche.
  604 Dress with brown top; white skirt; white and brown tam.
  605 Multi-colored polka dots on white dress; blue neck inset; straw hat with red ribbon.
  606 Blue jumper with red checked top; red straw hat.
  607 Red and white striped sailor dress; white and red tam.
  608 Blue organdy party dress with light lavender trim; blue straw hat trimmed with matching flowers.
Left to right: Row 3
  701 Summer dress with red top; print skirt with matching sleeves; navy blue straw hat trimmed with flowers.

264.

702 Scotch plaid in red and blue; matching plaid tam.

703 Yellow and blue print dress with large blue collar; natural straw hat trimmed with flowers.

704 High-waisted dress with red and white striped skirt and solid red top; red straw hat trimmed with ribbon.

705 Combination dress with yellow print skirt and blue top; yellow straw hat trimmed with matching flowers.

706 Dress with blue and pink plaid skirt and white top; white and navy blue tam.

707 Pink dress trimmed with white print braid; pink straw hat.

708 Lavender print dress trimmed with lace; matching straw hat trimmed with flowers.

Left to right: Row 4

801 Blue and white print sunsuit; glasses; matching blue hair ribbon.

802 Playsuit with blue jeans and red and white checkered shirt; red straw hat; glasses.

803 Traditional Scotch Lassie costume; green and red plaid skirt; black suit coat and Scotch hat with feather; large red purse.

804 Bedtime costume with pink, blue and green robe.

805 Lounging outfit with blue pants; yellow metallic wrap-around top; gold shoes; blue hair ribbon.

806 Pink ballerina costume; pink ballerina shoes; pink hair ribbon.

807 Light blue ice skating costume trimmed with a ruffle; pink puff hair piece.

808 Red and white ski outfit with matching hat; ski boots.

Left to right: Row 5

809 Red and white polka dot dress; matching plain red hat.

810 White coat and hat trimmed with black.

811 Yellow raincoat with hood; red ribbons for braided hair.

812 Blue coat with blue and white checked trim on collar and hat.

901 Bridal gown with long veil; bouquet.

902 Blue party dress; white fur stole and hat.

903 Rose dress with lace trim; white fur coat and tam.

Left to right: Row 6

907 Gift box with assorted clothes and accessories.

908 Red wardrobe trunk with doll included in red and white striped dress trimmed in blue; clothes, accessories and extra shoes included.

Left to right: Row 7

915, 916, 917, 918, 919, 920 Accessories in plastic and boxed containers.

921 Undressed *Muffie* with some of her wardrobes.

SEE: *Illustration 263.* Nancy Ann brochure.

Illustration 264. Nancy Ann brochure.

PRICE: $115-125 up for doll and mint outfit

$25-55 for unopened boxed outfit

The Nancy Ann company was sold to Albert Bourla and stockholders and they made an "International Series" which was introduced at the American Toy Fair in New York in 1967. Hong Kong was rapidly becoming the center of doll manufacturing and the clothes for this series were made there.

This doll was not in production very long because children wanted the teenage dolls. Although it is different from the other *Muffie* dolls, it has a charm of its own and is rare. (See Identification Guide, page 241.)

MARKS: None (doll)

Spanish Muffie: HP; 8in (20cm); head-turning walker with plastic mechanism; beautiful skin tone but different from earlier Nancy Ann dolls; mouth painted inside lines to make it appear smaller; eyelashes painted under eyes; legs wider and heavier than other Nancy Ann dolls; one line on seat; dressed in red taffeta with black lace and gold braid trim; lace mantilla with crown-like pseudo comb in front holding it up; gold earrings; black underclothes; stockings and shoes; all original, (see Identification Guide, page 241); 1967.

MARKS: None (doll)

SEE: *Illustration 265* (Color Section, page 165).

PRICE: $80-100 (The price of this doll has been rising because it is difficult to find.)

Around the World Muffie: HP; 8in (20cm); (for general characteristics, see *Illustration 265*); packed in see-through package; 1967.

MARKS: None (doll)

SEE: *Illustration 266. Chree M. Kysar Collection.*

PRICE: $80-100

266.

Debbie was made in both all-HP and HP with a vinyl head. Nancy Ann, following the general trend, introduced vinyl heads in the *Muffie, Debbie* and "Style Show" lines in the mid and later 1950s. This book shows the HP *Debbie. Debbie* with the vinyl head was shown in *Head Plastic Dolls, I,* page 191.

The HP *Debbie's* arm hooks are shown in this book in the Identification Guide, page 235. The arm hooks of *Debbie* with the vinyl head are shown in *Hard Plastic Dolls, I,* page 268U.

MARKS: "Nancy Ann" (head)

267.

Debbie: HP; 10½in (27cm); molded hair under lovely long blonde wig; jointed at neck, shoulders and hips; knees are not jointed; head turning walker; closed mouth; sleep eyes with molded lashes; heavy dark painted lashes under eyes; individual fingers; blue checked cotton dress; organdy apron with pink rickrack trim; yellow straw hat; pink plastic purse with "Debbie//By//Nancy Ann" printed on it; white slip attached to dress; 1955.

> **MARKS:** "Nancy Ann" in raised letters on back of head; these letters wear off easily; dress tag says, "Styled By Nancy Ann//Nancy Ann Storybook Dolls Inc.// San Francisco, California"
>
> **SEE:** *Illustration 267. Marge Meisinger Collection.*
>
> **PRICE:** $65-85

Debbie: clothes

> Left: pink coat; blue taffeta dress; blue shoes and socks; white fur piece and muff; white cotton panties; clothes in small Nancy Ann pink box with large polka dots; dress and coat not tagged.
>
> Right: satin bride dress with lace trim; net veil; bouquet of flowers; white satin slippers; white cotton panties; dress has Nancy Ann tag; large blue polka dot Nancy Ann box.
>
> **MARKS:** "Storybook Dolls by Nancy Ann//Debbie's Special Occasion Styles" (boxes)
>
> **SEE:** *Illustration 267. Marge Meisinger Collection.*
>
> **PRICE:** $25-50 (boxed outfit)

Debbie: HP; 10½in (27cm); according to the advertisement, the dolls were "Big and Little Sister dolls with look-alike costumes;" outfits could be purchased separately. There were over 60 different "look-alike" costumes; 1955.

> **SEE:** *Illustration 268. Playthings, August 1955.*

Roy Rogers and **Dale Evans:** HP; 8in (29cm); excellent quality dolls; medium dark skin tone; standard arm hooks (see Identification Guide, *Hard Plastic Dolls, I,* page 265K); feet like small Nancy Ann Storybook Dolls but no shoes painted on; dressed in Rodeo costumes; Nancy Ann gripper snaps (see Identification Guide, page 247); *Roy* has tan chaps; jeans; red, white, green and yellow plaid shirt; ears that stand away from head; lariat around wrist; *Dale* has same shirt; suede skirt; brown suede boots with yellow painted trim; Nancy Ann panties; both dolls have white cowboy hats; 1955.

268.

It's Roy and Dale!

270.

MARKS: None (dolls)
     "Nancy Ann Storybook Dolls Inc. of California 3R Roy Rogers" (box)
     "Nancy Ann Storybook Dolls Inc. of California 3D Dale Evans" (box)
SEE: *Illustration 269* (Color Section, page 221). *Nancy Catlin Collection.*
PRICE: $100-125 each; (rare dolls — very few sample prices)

Roy Rogers and **Dale Evans:** HP; 8in (20cm); advertisement says, "Every detail of clothing is authentic 'Roy Rogers' right down to the boots, belts and Roy and Dale's famous white felt hats. Three different surefire 'western' outfits: *Rodeo, Roundup* and *Parade;*" walkers; real eyelashes; dolls pictured are wearing rodeo outfits.
 SEE: *Illustration 270. Playthings,* July 1955.
 PRICE: $100-125 each

157

Nancy Ann Style Show Series **Brochure:** all-HP.

    MARKS: None (body and head); silver tag on wrist which listed the name of the doll
        and told of other available *Style Show* Dolls.
  SEE: *Illustration 271.* Nancy Ann brochure.
      Illustration 272. Nancy Ann brochure.
  PRICE: $400-475

271.

272.

The beautiful Nancy Ann *Style Show* doll is very popular with collectors. The clothing is beautifully designed and made. The *Style Show* doll is usually all-HP and it is rarely seen with a vinyl head mint-in-box. Since it is not marked, it is difficult to identify. This late 1950s' doll still has lovely material and costume design. The gripper snap matches the material (see Identification Guide, page 247).

MARKS: "18V" (head); none (body); "2403" (bottom of box and also inside box)

Nancy Ann Style Show Doll: HP with vinyl head; 18in (46cm); sleep eyes; closed mouth; same general body characteristics as all-HP doll; color on knees and wrists; 2nd and 3rd fingers molded together and curved forward; head-turning walker; excellent details on hands, wrists and ears; beautiful rooted hair; blue dress taffeta with lace trim on skirt and sleeves; rose sash and skirt trim; hat trimmed with flowers and wide rose ribbon; same underwear as used on the all-HP doll; stockings; gripper snaps (see *Illustration 424*, left).

MARKS: "18V" (head); none (body); "2403" (bottom of box, also inside box)
SEE: *Illustration 273* (Color Section, page 164). *Nancy Arches Collection.*
PRICE: $300-400 (very few sample prices available)

The world of *Nancy Ann Storybook Dolls* is a wonderful place for collectors. Not only were there different types of bodies and series, but the actual material was changed as Nancy Ann coped with changes and shortages. The different body styles were shown in *Hard Plastic Dolls, I.* This book shows a few of the intricate variations of dolls in a single series. A collector can pursue these dolls for years and continue to find beautiful new models. They also can store these dolls in a very small space. No wonder they are popular!

274.

Sisters Go to Sunday School: HP; *Little Sisters* all 3½in (9cm); black pupil sleep eyes; *Big Sister* is 5in (13cm); black pupil sleep eyes; all have high white boots. *Big* and *Little Sisters* always had matching dresses. However, the material among different sets of dolls varied, even within a one-year-period.

> SEE: *Illustration 274. Marianne Gardner Collection.*
> PRICE: $35-55 each

275.

Little Sisters Go to School: HP; 3½in (9cm); black pupil sleep eyes. This shows the progress and change in the plastic of one type of doll. The doll on the left has a very clear hard plastic. The second and third dolls each are more waxy. The doll on the right has a very yellow waxy hard plastic. The two dolls on the left are wearing the same dress. One is red and white; the other is green and white. The second doll from the right has a pale blue dress and the dress of the doll on the right is red and white.

> SEE: *Illustration 275. Marianne Gardner Collection.*
> PRICE: $35-55 each

continued on page 169

Ideal *Betsy McCall.*
(see page 137).

American Character
Sweet Alice (see page 44).

Effanbee *Honey Tintair* (see page 105). *Pat Parton Collection.*

Nancy Ann *Style Show* doll with vinyl head (see page 159). *Pat Arches Collection.*

Nancy Ann International *Muffie* (see page 155).

Effanbee *Honey Bride* (see page 106).

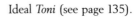

Ideal *Toni* (see page 135).

Cosmopolitan *Ginger Mouseketeer* (see page 80). *Marge Meisinger Collection.*

Rosebud *Miss Rosebud* (see page 199). *Virginia Heyerdahl Collection.*

Arranbee *Littlest Angel* in jodhpurs (see page 59).

Mary Hoyer *Bride* (see page 126). *Pat Parton
Collection.*

continued from page 160

Easter Dolls: HP; 5in (13cm); the doll on left is a painted-eye pinch face, circa 1948-1950 doll; the other two dolls are painted-eye dolls, circa 1951; all are dressed in cream-colored taffeta with tiny flowered print; large garden-type straw hats with a rose on top. Nancy Ann occasionally made special boxes for holiday dolls as can be seen in this illustration.

SEE: *Illustration 276. Marianne Gardner Collection.*

PRICE: $35-55 each

276.

Over the Rainbow #409: HP; 6in (15cm); painted eye; from "All-Time Hit Parade Series;" dressed in pink with black lace.

Maytime: HP; 6in (15cm); painted eye; #302 from "Operetta Series." The 300 and 400 series were quite elaborately dressed. Most of them had large hats.

SEE: *Illustration 277. Marianne Gardner Collection.*

PRICE: $35-55 each

277.

Beauty: HP; 5in (13cm); painted-eye pinch face; #156 orange organza dress with lace and orange metallic stripe around skirt; from *Beauty and the Beast.* (doll on left)

See Saw Marjory Daw: HP; 5in (13cm); painted-eye pinch face; #177 white taffeta dress with gold metallic stripes. (doll on right) There were many metallic fabrics used in this series.

SEE: *Illustration 278. Marianne Gardner Collection.*

PRICE: $35-55 each

278.

169

Niresk Industries, Inc.

The registered trademarks, the trademarks and the copyrights appearing in italics within this chapter belong to Niresk Industries, Inc., unless otherwise noted.

This Chicago marketing company was one of the largest sellers of dolls in the United States. They advertised in hobby and so-called "pulp" magazines in the 1950s. They purchased dolls from the original doll manufacturers and sold them at low cost. They imitated the more expensive dolls. Usually the dolls were not marked. Look-alike dolls included the Vogue *Ginny*®, Alexander ballerinas, Ideal *Saucy Walker*® and many, many others. Their advertisements continued into the advent of the high-heeled vinyl dolls.

Nina Ballerina: HP body with vinyl head; 20in (51cm); rooted Saran hair; sleep eyes; jointed at neck, shoulders and hips; thigh-length hose; frothy net skirt; gleaming lamé bodice spangled with sequins; Capezio ballet slippers; does splits and high kicks; see *Hard Plastic Dolls, I,* page 72, 1955.

SEE: *Illustration 279. Workbasket,* November 1955.
PRICE: $50-75

279.

Hollywood Bride with Seven-Outfit Trousseau: HP body with vinyl head; 18in (46cm); rooted hair; sleep eyes; walking doll; jointed at neck, shoulders and hips; outfits include coat and beret, hostess gown, ballerina, plastic raincoat, sheer nightgown and afternoon dress; 1955.

    SEE: *Illustration 280. Workbasket*, November 1955.

    PRICE: $50-75

280.

281.

Janie Pigtails: HP; 8in (20cm); Saran wig, head-turning walker; sleep eyes with real lashes; fully jointed; wardrobe and accessories available; hair can be styled to suit her costume; *Ginny*® look-alike; 1953. This advertisement should be compared with the Plastic Molded Arts *Joannie Pigtails*® advertisement in *Playthings*, March 1953; (see *Illustration 293*).

    MARKS: None (doll)

    SEE: *Illustration 281. Movieland*, October 1953

    PRICE: $25-35

Ginny® is a registered trademark of Vogue Dolls, Inc.
Joannie Pigtails® is a registered trademark of P.M.A., Inc.

171

Norma Originals, Inc.

The registered trademarks, the trademarks and the copyrights appearing in italics within this chapter belong to Norma Originals, Inc.

282.

283.

284.

Majorette: HP; 7½in (19cm); jointed at arms and neck; mitten hands; dressed as majorette with baton and plumed hat; 1951.

> MARKS: None (doll)
> SEE: *Illustration 282. Playthings,* March 1951.
> PRICE: $12-15

Norma Bride: HP; 8in (20cm); beautiful wig of long curly red hair; sleep eyes with molded lashes; no lashes painted on doll; standard arm hook; jointed at neck, shoulders and hips; molded-on slipper shoe with white only around bottom of shoe and not on straps (unusual) (see Identification Guide, page 252); lovely satin bride dress trimmed with lace; net veil with ornate lace; flowers at wrist; characteristics of Fortune and Virga dolls (see page 112); exceptional quality doll; mid 1950s.

> MARKS: None (doll); "A Norma Original" (wrist tag)
> SEE: *Illustration 283. Marge Meisinger Collection.*
> PRICE: $35-40

Martha Washington: HP; 7½in (19cm); jointed at arms and neck; PMA characteristics (page 177) except that it has mitten hands; rose colonial dress; blonde wig; educational story came with doll; circa early 1950s. Brochure in box says that there was a "Fact and Fiction Series," "International Series," "Bridal Series," "American Series," "Sport Series" and a "Petite Series" which were only 5½in (14cm) tall.

> MARKS: None (doll)
> SEE: *Illustration 284.*
> PRICE: $15

Groom: HP; 7½in (19cm); (see Fortune characteristics, page 112); painted-on black shoes (see Identification Guide, *Hard Plastic Dolls, I*, page 285H); black felt suit with white felt vest; rayon tie; black top hat; all original; circa early 1950s. The Norma company made very unusual and attractive boxes.

    MARKS: None (doll); "Norma Originals//Made to be loved//104 The Groom" (box)

SEE: *Illustration 285.*

PRICE: $20

285.

Old Cottage Toys

The registered trademarks, the trademarks and the copyrights appearing in italics within this chapter belong to Old Cottage Toys.

    During World War II it was difficult to get dolls for children. Mrs. M. E. Fleischmann started to make dolls for her daughter and by the end of the war, she was making dolls commercially. At first she used whatever materials were available. By 1948 Mrs. Fleischmann registered the trademark "Old Cottage Toys."

    Her daughter joined the company as co-owner when she grew up, and they employed talented craftsmen who used much handwork in the construction of both the dolls and the clothes. The clothes were well made with beautiful detail and a child could dress and undress the dolls. Soon the company developed a line of wonderful character dolls. Their 1970 catalog listed 56 different dolls. They were sold in Harrods and the Liberty department store in London and other leading stores in both England and the United States. The mail order firm of Mark Farmer in California also carried them.

    Their output never kept up with the demand and because of the handwork, the dolls were never inexpensive. As time passes, the dolls become more and more collectible. **GENERAL CHARACTERISTICS:** In the late 1940s Mrs. Fleischmann developed a compound with hard plastic characteristics which she used for the movable head of the doll. The faces were beautifully sculptured and the colors bright and lifelike. There was excellent detail in the hand-painted faces.

    The body was made of tightly stuffed, flesh-colored felt which was jointed with a special wire armature which allowed the head, arms and legs to move freely.

    An unusual characteristic of these dolls was the large flat feet which are so carefully balanced that the doll can stand with no other support.

The dolls originally came in 8in (20cm) to 9in (23cm) and 11in (28cm) to 12in (31cm) sizes when dressed, but later the larger dolls were dropped from the line. These larger dolls are now quite rare and valuable.

TYPES OF DOLLS: historical figures; fairy tale figures; nationality dolls; English characters including the *London Policeman, Guardsman, Pearly King* and *Queen*. Another favorite doll was the one-piece felt baby with blonde curls.

Probably the most popular were the Victorian children. Pam purchased one in Harrods on her first trip overseas when she was 16. Years later when she returned to England and Harrods, she was disappointed when the saleswoman told her that they were so scarce and expensive that they only sold them during the Christmas season.

DESIGN CENTRE OF LONDON: The Council of Industrial Design selects the finest crafts in production for exhibition at the Design Centre in London. These products are allowed to be tagged with the Design Centre label. Some of the Old Cottage Dolls carry this tag along with the tag printed with the registered trademark of the company.

Mrs. Fleischmann was commissioned by Metro-Goldwyn Mayer to make a Japanese doll representing the film *Teahouse of the August Moon* which appeared on the film's showcard. She also made a doll to promote the film *Gigi.* The British Broadcasting Company asked her to make characters for a television broadcast, and she made *Tweedledee* and *Tweedledum*, characters from *Alice Through the Looking Glass.*

PRESERVATION WARNING: Care should be taken with the storage of these dolls. The hard plastic-type material of the Old Cottage Dolls has been known to "collapse." The dolls should be placed away from direct sunlight, heat, cold, and so forth. However, so far this does not seem to be a common occurrence.

286.

Scotland Boy: HP-type head with felt body; 9in (23cm); unusually large feet and shoes; painted face; nicely sculptured head; three lashes on side of eye; Stuart plaid kilt, scarf, hatband and cuffs of shoes; black velvet jacket; lace jabot and cuffs.

MARKS: None (doll); picture of cottage with "Registered//Trade Mark" (tag); "Old// Cottage//Doll//Made in// England" (reverse side of tag)
SEE: *Illustration 286.*
PRICE: $70-95

Winter Girl in Kate Greenaway Style: (see page 173 for general characteristics); 9in (23cm); black flannel dress; blue brocade apron; white collar and cap trimmed in lace.

MARKS: See *Illustration 174.*
SEE: *Illustration 286.*
PRICE: $70-95

Amy: for general characteristics see page 173; 10in (25cm); dressed in blue dotted dress; white organdy apron; blonde pigtail wig; white shoes and socks; 1969. This doll was advertised in the 1971 Mark Farmer catalog.

MARKS: See *Illustration 286*; other tag says "as selected for the Design//Center//London"
SEE: *Illustration 287. Mary Elizabeth Poole Collection.*
PRICE: $85-110

Baby: entire doll one-piece felt; 4-3/4in (12cm); blonde curly wig; pink baby dress and matching bonnet; 1969.

MARKS: None
SEE: *Illustration 287. Mary Elizabeth Poole Collection.*
PRICE: $40-45

Goose Girl: for general characteristics, see page 173; red felt dress and shoes; print apron and matching kerchief; plastic goose.

SEE: *Illustration 288. Mary Elizabeth Poole Collection.*
PRICE: $85-95 (small doll)
$100-130 + (larger size)

287.

288.

Tweedledum and Tweedledee: 10in (25cm); for general characteristics, see page 173; unusually large head; English schoolboy uniform; royal blue felt shirt; beige felt pants; blue and beige felt cap; 1968. These dolls were made for the English British Broadcasting Company for a television broadcast. They were schoolboy characters from *Through the Looking-Glass* by Lewis Carroll.

 MARKS: "Old Cottage Dolls" on tag; "Dee" and "Dum" written on the left shirt collar of each doll.

 SEE: *Illustration 289. Christine Lorman Collection.*

 PRICE: $600+ (very few sample prices available)

289.

Ontario Plastic Inc.

The registered trademarks, the trademarks and the copyrights appearing in italics within this chapter belong to Ontario Plastic, Inc., unless otherwise noted.

Paula Sue: HP; 8in (20cm); non-walking; sleep eyes with plastic eyelashes; deep clefts under nose; no painted eyelashes; arm hook similar to Vogue *Ginny* with squared-off plastic piece holding a metal ring (see Identification Guide, page 235); original clothes; white dress with multi-colored ribbon trim; unusual gripper snap closing (see Identification Guide, page 247); for body comparison with other 8in (20cm) (see Identification Guide, page 241); mid 1950s.

 MARKS: "Ontario Plastic Inc.// Rochester N. Y." (back)

 SEE: *Illustration 290. Marge Meisinger Collection.*

 PRICE: $20-25

290.

Ginny® is a registered trademark of Vogue Dolls, Inc.

P & M Doll Company

THE DOLL THAT DOES EVERYTHING!
- SITS!
- KNEELS!
- BENDS!
- WALKS!

P & M's
Paula Mae
MAGIC
KNEE ACTION DOLL
•
WHITE & COLORED DOLLS
Our Brand New
ALL VINYL CREATIONS

are consistent in every way with the fine quality our customers have come to expect from P&M. And, of course, all beautifully costumed in the P&M manner, in keeping with the prevailing trend in infants' attire. Here, indeed, quality predominates, though the retail prices are designed to produce volume sales.

We are featuring All Vinyl Dolls and also our Paula Mae Walking Doll

291.

Paula Mae Magic Knee Action Doll: HP body with vinyl head; rooted hair; *Saucy Walker®* look-alike; sits, kneels, bends and walks; 1955.

   SEE: *Illustration 291. Playthings,* March 1955.

   PRICE: $50-60 (white doll)
   $65-80 (black doll)

Saucy Walker® is a registered trademark of the Ideal Toy Corp.

P.M.A. Dolls, Inc. (Plastic Molded Arts)

Plastic Molded Arts was a company which marketed many inexpensive dolls during the 1950s. Many of these dolls were featured in *Hard Plastic Dolls, I,* pages 207-211. This book shows illustrations of the *Ginny®*-type dolls by PMA which were not pictured in the earlier book.

Although there are none of these inexpensive small "fashion and character" type dolls in this book, as a convenience to the reader, the characteristics of these dolls are repeated below.

PMA Characteristics:
1. Double triangle mouth.
2. Molded eyelashes.
3. Heavy eyelashes beneath eyes.
4. Ear mold runs through ear.
5. 2nd and 3rd fingers molded together.
6. Two lines on palm of hand.
7. The tiny early dolls often have eyelashes above eye and no molded or imitation eyelashes.
8. The great majority have sleep eyes.
9. Most of the dolls have the standard arm hook (see Identification Guide, *Hard Plastic Dolls, I,* page 264H).
10. Molded and painted shoes with bow detail. There are several different types (see *Hard Plastic Dolls, I,* page 283A, B and C for details on shoes).

Ginny® is a registered trademark of Vogue Dolls, Inc.

PMA Characteristics of Ginny®-type dolls:
1. Head-turning walkers.
2. Sleep eyes.
3. The early dolls have real eyelashes. The later dolls have molded eyelashes.
4. Washable Saran wigs on HP dolls; rooted, washable hair on vinyl-headed dolls.
5. Heavy painted eyelashes (usually around entire eye).
6. Molded-on slippers which are painted, unpainted or just the bottom part is painted toes.
7. Standard arm hook (see *Hard Plastic Dolls, I*, Identification Guide, page 264I).

Joanie Pigtails: HP; 8in (20cm); Saran wig; head turning walker; sleep eyes with real lashes; heavily painted eyelashes around entire eye; molded-on slipper shoes which are sometimes painted and sometimes left in natural color (see Identification Guide, *Illustration 431*); standard arm hook (see *Hard Plastic Dolls, I*, Identification Guide, page 264I); 1953.
Niresk Industries marketed a *Janie Pigtail®* during the same year using the same basic doll (see Illustration 281).
    MARKS: None (doll)
    SEE: *Illustration 292. Playthings*, March 1953.
    PRICE: $20-40 (depending on outfit)

Joanie Pigtails Wardrobe and Travel Case: HP; 8in (20cm); (for general characteristics, see *Illustration 292*); case include dress, panties, curlers, two-piece pajamas, shoes, mirror, comb and brush; not a walker; 1953.
    MARKS: None (doll)
    SEE: *Illustration 293. Playthings*, April 1953.
    PRICE: $35-40 +

Ginny® is a registered trademark of Vogue Dolls, Inc.

Janie Pigtails® is a registered trademark of Niresk Industries.

292.

293.

Joanie Walker: HP; 8in (20cm); (for general characteristics see page 178); molded slipper feet (see Identification Guide, page 252); pointed arched eyebrows; circa 1953.

> MARKS: None (doll); "Joanie Walker//P.M.A. Dolls, Inc" (box)
> SEE: *Illustration 294.*
> PRICE: $25-35

Joanie-the Wedding Belle: HP; 8in (20cm); (for general characteristics, see page 178); white satin wedding gown with matching panties; Saran wig; party dress and matching panties; pocketbook; comb; mirror; curlers; advertisement said, "Something old-bridal veil//something new-wedding slippers//something borrowed-wedding ring//something blue-wedding garter;" not a walker; 1953. *Joanie* came with a travel case with metal locks and a plastic handle.

> SEE: *Illustration 295. Playthings,* June 1953.
> PRICE: $35-40

294.

Stepping Steppers: HP; 11in (28cm); head turning walker; washable Saran wig; sleep eyes; wardrobe available; plain plastic shoes with plastic bow; 1953.

> SEE: *Illustration 296. Playthings,* March 1953.
> PRICE: $10-15

Here comes the Bride...

295.

296.

Chubby Type Girl: HP; 10½in (27cm); head turning walker; hidden pin walker (see *Hard Plastic Dolls, I*, page 291D); 2nd and 3rd fingers molded together; dimples on back of hands; toes all molded together; clothes not original; arm hook (see Identification Guide, page 236); circa mid 1950s.

MARKS: "Plastic Molded Arts Co.// L.I.C. New York" (back)
SEE: *Illustration 297. Helen M. Keefe Collection.*
PRICE: $20-30

297.

Miss Joan: HP; 12in (31cm); sleep eyes with eyelashes painted under eyes; jointed at neck, arms, hips and above knees; unusually nice doll; brunette hair; excellent skin color; arm hook (see Identification Guide, page 236); 2nd and 3rd fingers molded together and curving inward; all original; dressed in lace underwear with stockings and high-heeled shoes; circa 1957.

There are very few all-HP high-heeled dolls.

MARKS: "Pat's Pend." (doll); "Miss Joan 1200//P.M.A. Dolls Inc." (box)
SEE: *Illustration 298.*
PRICE: $25-35

298.

Little Miss Joan: HP; 9in (23cm); Saran wig; walking doll; jointed at neck, shoulders, hips and knees; high heeled; came with outfits to purchase separately including a mink stole; 1957.

This is an unusual size for a high-heeled doll, especially one with bent knees.

SEE: *Illustration 299. Toys and Novelties,* February 1957.

PRICE: $25-35

299.

Paris Doll Company

The registered trademarks, the trademarks and the copyrights appearing in italics within this chapter belong to Paris Doll Company, unless otherwise noted.

Rita Majorette: HP; 29in (74cm); walker; open mouth with teeth and felt tongue; lines above and below knees; dimples on knees; very "bulky" doll; *Mary Hartline®* look-alike; white majorette outfit trimmed with gold; circa early 1950s.

MARKS: None

SEE: *Illustration 300. Nancy Carlton Collection.*

PRICE: $125-150

Mary Hartline® is a registered trademark of the Ideal Toy Corp.

300.

Rita: HP; 29in (74cm); walking doll; (see *Illustration 300* for general characteristics); large "bulky" doll that can wear little girl dresses. The 1951 doll was all-hard plastic. Later the doll was made with a vinyl head and increased 2in (5.1cm) in size. (See *Illustration 302.*)

> MARKS: None (doll)
> SEE: *Illustration 301. Playthings,* March 1951.
> PRICE: $125-150

Rita: HP body with vinyl head; 31in (79cm); (see *Illustration 300* for general characteristics); rooted hair; dressed in red and white checked rayon taffeta dress with braid trimmed collar; short puffed sleeves; red plastic belt; red shoes.

> MARKS: None (body)
> SEE: *Illustration 302.* Marshall Field & Co. 1954 Christmas catalog. *Barbara Andresen Collection.*
> PRICE: $125-150

301.

302.

Pedigree Company Soft Toys Limited

The registered trademarks, the trademarks and the copyrights appearing in italics within this chapter belong to Pedigree Company Soft Toys Limited, unless otherwise noted.

The name "Pedigree" was first used in 1942 for dolls and toys made at the Triang Works at Merton, London, England. The company registered the name "Pedigree" as a trademark that year. They have issued a large line of dolls for a long time. During the 1950s many of their dolls were modeled after those made in the United States. Most of them have the Pedigree signature on the head.

The company was proud of their high standards of workmanship and made the entire dolls in their factory. Their clothing and accessories were also of high quality and lasted well through many hours of children's play.

During the 1950s they had several factories in England as well as one in Belfast, Northern Ireland. There were ten factories in Canada, South Africa and New Zealand. They not only made many dolls, but they had a line of toys, prams, tricycles, toy trains and many other things.

In addition to the dolls shown in this book, their line during these years included:

1. *Magic Skin* dolls
2. Hard plastic dolls with vinyl heads
3. A popular 10in (25cm) *Fairy* with a mohair wig and wand
4. A 19in (48cm) *Elizabeth* teenage-type doll which was produced for *Woman's Illustrated* magazine. The doll's clothes were designed by the magazine's fashion expert, Veronica Scott. Patterns could be purchased from the magazine.
5. A 20in (51cm) head-turning walking boy doll with flirty eyes and molded curly hair painted brown.
6. Black versions of their popular dolls
7. Well into the 1960s they made hard plastic *Tartan* dolls in 12in (31cm), 14in (36cm), 15in (38cm) and 17in (43cm) sizes. Some of the dolls had musical movements within their body.
8. In the 1960s they made hard plastic character dolls in such natural costumes as *Swiss Miss*, *Dutch Girl* and *Welsh Girl*. Other character dolls included *Red Riding Hood*, *Madame Butterfly*, *Chloe* (black doll), *Kathleen of Ireland*, *Tommy Atkins*, *Manuel the Matador* and *Abdul the Turk*.
9. Other character dolls included *Robin Hood*, *Mary Had a Little Lamb* and *Ride a Cock Horse*.

Little Princess: One of the most desirable Pedigree hard plastic dolls is the lovely *Little Princess* modeled after Princess Anne. She was featured in an article in the magazine *Woman's Illustrated.* She says, "My name is 'Little Princess.' I am a special doll because I'm the first doll in the land. Norman Hartnell, the Queen's Dressmaker has designed the pretty lace trimmed frock I am wearing. All the other dolls will be envious because Normal Hartnell has designed so many pretty clothes for me...Pierre Balmain has planned a Paris wardrobe of clothes for me, too."

    SEE: *Illustration 303. Mary Elizabeth Poole Collection.*
          Illustration 304. Mary Elizabeth Poole Collection.
    PRICE: No sample prices available.

Little Princess: HP; 14in (36cm); jointed at neck, shoulders and legs; blonde mohair wig; lovely color with red cheeks; sleep eyes; white and red dotted dress with red rickrack trim; all original; purchased by owner in 1953.

    SEE: *Illustration 305. Mary Elizabeth Poole Collection.*

304.

303.

305.

AN IRISH SKIRT AND SHAWL TO MAKE
Designed by Sybil Connolly of Dublin

YOU can make this pretty Irish skirt and shawl for "Little Princess" very easily. All you need is a piece of bright red, thin felt, 18 inches square. Now cut it into a circle (like the diagram below) which measures 18 inches across. Find the centre of the circle and cut out a round hole measuring 3½ inches across.

Cut a little slit down from the edge of this circle so that dolly can get into her skirt easily, and fasten opening with a hook and eye.

The shawl is made from a triangle of black woollen material (as in diagram 2), and you can trim it very prettily with wool fringing, that Mummy can make or buy for you.

TWO PIECES . . .
NO SEAMS . . .

306.

307.

308.

Little Princess Pattern: An Irish Skirt and Shawl to Make; Designed by Sybil Connolly of Dublin; 1953.

> SEE: *Illustration 306. Woman's Illustrated,* Special Design. *Mary Elizabeth Poole Collection.*

Doll in Knit Outfit: HP; 22in (56cm); head-turning walker; flirty eyes; washable wig; grill in stomach; open mouth with teeth; pin-jointed walker with unpainted Ideal screw-type pin (see Identification Guide, *Hard Plastic Dolls, I,* page 290B); individual fingers; painted eyelashes under eyes; *Saucy Walker®*-type; circa 1953.

The English people wear their "woolies" for most of the year. Knitting is still popular and mothers and grandmothers make many doll clothes for the children. Because of this, it is sometimes difficult to find original clothes on English dolls. This wonderful doll has a complete knitted outfit including outer wrap, dress, full slip, separate undershirt, panties and shoes. She was purchased in Warwick, England.

> MARKS: "Pedigree//England" (head)
> SEE: *Illustration 307.*
> PRICE: $80-90

Pin-Up Doll: HP; 14in (36cm); "Magic Nylon" blonde hair; face slightly different from the Ideal *Toni®* doll but the body is almost the same; skin tone darker and brighter; bright red cheeks which are traditional with English dolls; Ÿ on backside; came with "Pin-Up Play Perm Wave Kit," creme shampoo; 1952. There were six dolls in different "teenage" dresses.

> MARKS: "Pedigree//Made in England" (head)
> SEE: *Illustration 308. Pat Parton Collection.*
> PRICE: $65-85 (in original clothes)

Saucy Walker® is a registered trademark of the Ideal Toy Corp.
Toni® is a registered trademark of The Gillette Co.

309.

Costume Dolls: European HP; 6½in (15cm); sleep eyes with hand-painted lashes above eyes; no molded lashes; pretty faces; non-walkers; doll on left has shoes and socks painted over the mold; doll on right has no paint on feet. These dolls were sold to companies in European countries as well as in Great Britain who dressed them in provincial outfits and sold them as "tourist" dolls in their own country. These dolls are of excellent quality.

    MARKS: "Made in England" (body)
    SEE: *Illustration 309. Marge Meisinger Collection.*
    PRICE: $30-35

Delite Doll: HP; 7in (18cm); jointed at neck and arms only; blue sleep eyes with no lashes; molded non-painted hair; mitten hands with deep dimples above each finger; "Precision moulding for true to life definition of limbs; modelled by a sculptor — a specialist in doll design" (printed on side of box); 1950s.

    MARKS: "Pedigree (in triangle//Made in//England" (back); "Pedigree Delite Dolls" (box)
    SEE: *Illustration 310.*
    PRICE: $6-7 (in box)

310.

Toddler: HP; (22cm); wind-up walking doll; circa 1953.

    SEE: *Illustration 311. Woman's Illustrated. Mary Elizabeth Poole Collection.*

311.

Pressman Toy Corp.

Fever Doll with Hospital Bed: HP; 7in (18cm); part of doctor-nurse set; painted eyes; open mouth for thermometer; mechanism to make face red on inside of jaw; jointed arms and legs only; bed is 8½in (22cm); bed fully HP; windup crank operates a hospital bed, came in doctor-nurse sets; circa 1955.

Advertisement says, "This super-realistic Doctor-Nurse-Small Fry Hospital set featuring the Fever Doll — a 'patient' that actually runs a temperature and gets red in the face when lowered on the adjustable hospital bed."

MARKS: "Pressman Toy Corporation//Made in U.S.A.//Pat. Pend." (doll)
SEE: *Illustration 312.* (left)
      Illustration 313. Playthings, March 1955. (right)
PRICE: $25 (for working set)

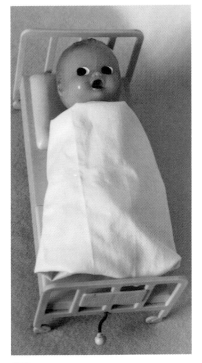

312.

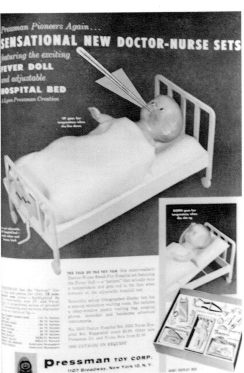

313.

187

Reina Doll Corp.

The registered trademarks, the trademarks and the copyrights appearing in italics within this chapter belong to Reina Doll Corp.

Best Dressed Doll in America: HP; 13in (33cm); fully jointed; mohair wigs; hand-painted faces; packed individually in gift window box; 1950.

    SEE: *Illustration 314. Playthings,* March 1950.

    PRICE: $15-25

314.

Reliable Toy Co. Ltd./Ltee (Canada)

The registered trademarks, the trademarks and the copyrights appearing in italics within this chapter belong to Reliable Toy Co. Ltd/ Ltee.

Established in 1920 in Toronto, Canada, the Reliable Toy Co. has a long tradition of making fine dolls. Originally they manufactured stuffed animals but in 1933 they started to make dolls. In that year they made a *Shirley Temple* doll.

Through World War II the company made composition dolls. Two of their most popular were *Maggie Muggins* and Olympic champion ice skater *Barbara Ann Scott.*

According to Mr. L. S. Samuels, the hard plastic or injection mold process dolls were excellent dolls but expensive to make. Reliable made the doll bodies themselves, and they have been one of the few doll makers on this continent to continue this rather than relying on foreign makers.

Probably their most famous doll during the hard plastic era was the *Queen Elizabeth II* doll made for the coronation. (See page 94.)

Plassikins: HP; 15in (38cm); head-turning hip-pin walker with painted outside pins (see Identification Guide, *Hard Plastic Dolls, I*, page 290A); sleep eyes with molded lashes; open/closed mouth with two painted teeth; excellent color with rosy cheeks; diamond seat pattern (see Identification Guide, *Hard Plastic Dolls, I*, page 282A); all original pink glazed cotton dress and hat; brown shoes; circa 1954.

    MARKS: "Reliable" in script (back)

    SEE: *Illustration 315* (Color Section, page 224).

    PRICE: $55-80

Dress-Me Doll: HP; 12in (31cm); sleep eyes; very pointed eyebrows; jointed at neck and shoulders only; wig; four fingers molded together; sold in sealed plastic bags; circa 1956-1962.

MARKS: "Reliable" (back)
"Reliable//all plastic//Dress Me Doll//Sleeping Eyes// Movable head and arms; Reliable Toy Co. Limited// Toronto.Montreal.Vancouver." (cardboard at top of plastic bag)

SEE: *Illustration 316. Elsie Ogden Collection.*

PRICE: $10-15

Indian: dark HP; 11in (28cm); gold flannel Indian outfit; multi-colored braid trim and headband; sleep brown eyes; molded lashes; small tuft of mohair attached to front of painted molded hair; circa mid 1950s.

MARKS: "Reliable//Made in Canada" (body)

SEE: *Illustration 317. Pat Parton Collection.*

PRICE: $25-30

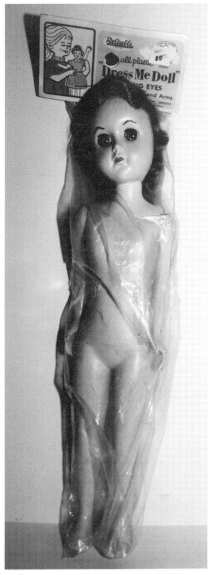

316.

 317.

Richwood Toys, Inc.

The Richwood Enterprises Company was located in Annapolis, Maryland, and made a *Ginny*-type doll before *Ginny* was named. *Sandra Sue* dates from the late 1940s to the late 1950s. Her beautiful wardrobe followed the style changes of the period.

Sandra Sue was made first with a flat foot to accommodate little girl and sports clothes. Later she was made with a high-heeled foot when the mature fashions were popular. (See Identification Guide, page 239.) Like the Alexander *Elise* doll with the jointed foot and the Cosmopolitan *Ginger* with the *Cha Cha Heel*, the *Sandra Sue* doll offered a choice to mothers who were concerned about the new mature dolls.

The following features were advertised:
1. Slender figure designed for stylish clothes.
2. Ball jointed and can sit, stand, move her head and arms.
3. Walking doll with a smooth all-metal mechanism.
4. A beautiful face created by a famous sculptor (possibly Agop Agopoff).
5. Moving eyes with tiny eyelashes.
6. Hand-decorated face with a different expression on each doll.
7. Saran wig which is stitchblocked, durable, washable and combable.
8. Porcelain-like finish specially processed on all parts.
9. A hospitalization policy which gave an exclusive lifetime guarantee of unbreakability.
10. A playworld of clothes, furniture, accessories and play equipment scaled just for her.

Sandra Sue Skater: HP; 8in (20cm); walker head does not turn; sleep eyes; highly arched, thin, dark orange eyebrows and eyelashes below the eyes; closed mouth; thin legs; flat feet; 1st, 2nd and 3rd fingers molded together; Ÿ on seat; loop arm hook (see Identification Guide, *Hard Plastic Dolls, I*, page 263F); all original clothes; red flannel skating skirt and pants; blue knit sweater with white over sweater trimmed with braid; white mittens; red stockinette cap; white skates; red knee socks; blonde hair; mid 1950s.
   MARKS: "2" (inside of right arm); "0" (inside of left arm)
   SEE: *Illustration 318* (Color Section, page 220).
   PRICE: $65-80

Louisa May Alcott Dolls, Beth, Amy, Marmee, Meg and *Jo:* the company brochure says "The charm and wholesomeness of the real life story of Louisa May Alcott's 'Little Women' make it a favorite of girls today just as it was one of mine. It gives me great pleasure to present my interpretaion of the unforgettable characters of Marmee, Meg, Beth, Amy, and Jo in the wonderful book for today's little women."
   SEE: *Illustration 319*. Company brochure from *Kathryn Davis Collection*.
   PRICE: $65-75 each (without box)
          $80-100 each (with box)

319.

Sandra Sue Brochure:

"Sandra Sue's trim little figure with its tiny waistline makes it possible for her to have clothes styled in fashions suitable for both the pre-teenage girl and the glamorous young lady. All of her coats have the fitted waist and flared skirts so popular this season.

"Sandra can look so grownup in her beautiful evening gowns and bridal outfits. She can look like a real little girl in her pretty short dresses or her winter sports clothes."

SEE: *Illustration 320.* Richwood Company brochure from *Kathryn Davis Collection.*

PRICE: $25-50 (outfits mint-in-zippered plastic bag)

320.

Sandra Sue Brochure:
Variety is the spice of life, and *Sandra Sue* had an outfit for every occasion. All of the designs in *Sandra Sue's* wardrobe were styles which America's best-dressed little girls were wearing in the 1950s.

SEE: *Illustration 321.* Company brochure from *Kathryn Davis Collection.*

321.

Sandra Sue Brochure:
SEE: *Illustration 322.* Company brochure from *Kathryn Davis Collection.*

322.

Sandra Sue: (for general characteristics, see page 190). This doll was advertised in *Hobbies* magazine. It suggested that this early high-heeled doll was not only a play doll, but it was also an excellent collector's item.

SEE: *Illustration 323. Hobbies,* March and April 1958. *Marge Meisinger Collection.*

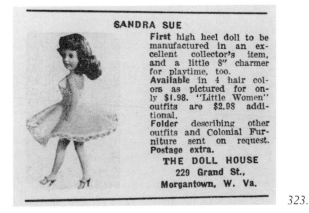

SANDRA SUE

First high heel doll to be manufactured in an excellent collector's item, and a little 8″ charmer for playtime, too.
Available in 4 hair colors as pictured for only $1.98. "Little Women" outfits are $2.98 additional.
Folder describing other outfits and Colonial Furniture sent on request. Postage extra.

THE DOLL HOUSE
229 Grand St.,
Morgantown, W. Va.

323.

Sandra Sue: This lovely doll had a beautiful extensive wardrobe. Today these tiny clothes are hard to identify. The following clothes were sold on a hanger in a plastic zippered bag. Accessories were sold in a round plastic container.

1. Accessories: white hat and shoes with various colored jewelry.
   SEE: *Illustration 324. Elsie Ogden Collection.*
   PRICE: $15-20
2. Formal dress: green taffeta long dress trimmed with lavender flowers.
   SEE: *Illustration 325. Elsie Ogden Collection.*
   PRICE: $15-20
3. Playsuit: white top with red shorts.
   SEE: *Illustration 326. Elsie Ogden Collection.*
   PRICE: $15-20

324.   325.   326.

Sandra Sue Furniture: "Sandra Sue is proud to be the only doll for whom a complete authentic set of furniture has been designed. The early Colonial homes of historic Annapolis have been the inspiration for this beautiful furniture."

1. Top: genuine mahogany Duncan Phyfe extension table with matching chairs. The table seats four dolls without leaf and six with leaf. The chairs are covered in a provincial print.
2. Left: the mahogany-finish tester bed is almost 12in (31cm) long and comes complete with canopy, bedspread, pillow, pillowcase and mattress. The canopy, bedspread and pillow are of crisp white material. All materials are washable.
3. Right: the 12in (31cm) solid mahogany wardrobe contains a shelf for hats and a hanging bar with tiny hangers for ensembles of clothes.

The *Sandra Sue* dolls were made in Annapolis, Maryland.

    SEE: *Illustration 327.* Company brochure from *Kathryn Davis Collection.*

327.

Sandra Sue Furniture Not Pictured:

1. Mahogany chest-on-chest with brass-handled drawers that open.
2. Mahogany vanity and stool with white dimity skirts; mirror.
3. Mahogany bureau with mirror; brass handles; drawers that open.
4. Bright red sliding board with ladder and silver sliding surface.

Additional Clothes Not Pictured: stylish clothes for high-heeled doll (circa 1956-1957).

1. Afternoon dress of powder puff muslin print with wide sash; straw hat.
2. Two-piece nylon polka dot short bridesmaid dress; nylon petticoat; bouquet.
3. Two-piece gold print afternoon party dress with jewel trim; straw hat.
4. Sophisticated evening gown with very full white nylon skirt and strapless red and silver bodice. (See *Hard Plastic Dolls, I*, page 216, *Illustration 473.*)
5. Jewel-trimmed black taffeta tea dance dress; matching hat. (See *Hard Plastic Dolls, I*, page 216, *Illustration 473a.*)
6. Nylon embroidered organdy party dress; matching straw lace hat.
7. Two-piece dress with sheer white nylon top and velvet skirt.
8. Checked taffeta suit with ruffled petticoat; separate jacket; straw hat.
9. Blue jeans with plaid cuffs; matching plaid shirt; white sailor hat.
10. Scotch suit with authentic details; wool jacket; plaid tartan and garters.
11. Bathing suit of jersey with satin panel; beach hat; terry cloth beach jacket.
12. Two-tone organdy party dress with lace trim; contrasting sash and flowers.
13. Velvet and gold tea dance dress; white taffeta petticoat; gold Juliet cap.

Tina Sue: NOT PHOTOGRAPHED (circa 1956-57): *Tina Sue* is an 8in (20cm) jointed soft vinyl baby doll; sparkling sleep eyes with tiny lashes; came with diapers and booties. A spool cradle could be purchased separately.

Cindy Lou: painted HP; 14in (36cm); head-turning walker; pin-jointed knees; auburn wig; beautiful flesh tones; sleep eyes with lashes; arm hooks (see Identification Guide, page 236); painted fingernails; medium blue felt lined skirt, jacket, pants; pink top and gloves; skates are attached to shoes; advertised in December 1951 *House and Garden* magazine; original price was $11.20. Although the brochure says the doll is 14in (36cm), it actually measures almost 15in (38cm).

> MARKS: "Made In U.S.A." in circle (back); box shows a picture of a clock with "Cindy Lou" written across it. Around the clock is "Round the Clock Doll Fashions//Highland, Maryland"
>
> SEE: *Illustration 328. Marge Meisinger Collection.*
>
> PRICE: $85-115 (in original clothes)

Cindy Lou "Round the Clock Fashions":

1. Blue taffeta dress with blue velvet trim; gold shoes.
2. Red calico skirt; white top with red rickrack trim; white cotton petticoat.

Clothes came in see-through plastic top box with the clock logo in the lower right corner.

> MARKS: "Round the Clock Fashions" (on box)
>
> SEE: *Illustration 329. Marge Meisinger Collection.*
>
> PRICE: $20-30 (boxed outfit)

328.

329.

Cindy Lou Round the Clock Fashion Brochure:
SEE: *Illustration 330. Marge Meisinger Collection.*

330.

SEE: *Illustration 331. Marge Meisinger Collection.*

331.

SEE: *Illustration 332. Marge Meisinger Collection.*

332.

Roberta Doll Co., Inc.

The registered trademarks, the trademarks and the copyrights appearing in italics within this chapter belong to Roberta Doll Co., Inc.

The Roberta Doll Company was one of the early companies in the hard plastic field. In 1950 they were offering all plastic character dolls, girl dolls, bride dolls and baby dolls (featuring plastic heads with latex and vinyl arms and legs). That year they introduced *Baby Babette*.

SEE: *Illustration 333. Playthings,* March 1950.

333.

Rosebud (England)

The Rosebud Company began after World War II. They started with composition dolls but by 1950 they were making baby dolls of hard plastic which were sent around the world until the mid 1960s. *Woman's Weekly* magazine featured *Rosebud* twin dolls and knitted outfits that were designed for them. Readers could send to the magazine to purchase the doll.

Many sizes of dolls were made by injection molding (hard plastic method) from 6in (15cm) to 21in (53cm). However, many of the dolls were small. The famous beautiful Rosebud doll box was popular with English children everywhere.

Rosebud and Mattel of the United States began to work together in 1964 as each started with the pull string talking mechanism. Mattel took over Rosebud in 1967.

Chiltern was a company which marketed Rosebud dolls. Their coronation *Peeress* was issued in 1953 dressed in velvet and wearing a tiara. This was in honor of the Queen's coronation that year. (See Coronation Section, page 75 and Color Section, page 94.)

Baby: HP; 5½in (14cm); sleep eyes; molded hair; very rosy cheeks; Ÿ on backside; two dimples in each knee; unusual right hand construction; 2nd, 3rd and 4th fingers folded under which allows the baby to suck its thumb; left hand has individual fingers; doll was sent to owner from South Africa; 1950s to the mid 1960s. This was a very popular doll which was sold around the world. Stores in Sweden, in particular, sold many of these dolls.
    MARKS: "Rosebud//Made//In//England" (back)
    SEE: *Illustration 334. Virginia Ann Heyerdahl Collection.*
    PRICE: $15-25

Fairy Dolls: HP; 6½in (16cm); jointed at arms only; net dress with gold sparkle trim; Ÿ backside; sleep eyes; individual fingers; usually boxed in lovely Rosebud box; sent to the owner from South Africa; mid 1950s.
    MARKS: "Rosebud//Made in England//Patent Pending" (body)
    SEE: *Illustration 335. Virginia Ann Heyerdahl Collection.*
    PRICE: $25-35

334.

335.

Baby Rosebud Toddler: HP; 6½in (17cm); came in beautiful box; sold as a "Dress-Me" type of doll; mothers and grandmothers often crocheted or knitted "woolies" for this doll; mid 1950s.

MARKS: "Rosebud//Made in England//Patent Pending" (body)

SEE: *Illustration 336. Virginia Ann Heyerdahl Collection.*

PRICE: $25-35

336.

Miss Rosebud: HP; 7½in (19cm); painted eyelashes above sleep eyes; 3rd and 4th fingers joined together; non-walker; all original pink net dress with pink embroidery and blue net trim; pink underdress; parasol of same material and color; unusual medieval style dress; circa mid 1950s.

MARKS: "Miss Rosebud" (body); "Rosebud" (head)

SEE: *Illustration 337* (Color Section, page 167). *Virginia Ann Heyerdahl Collection.*

PRICE: $35-40

Miss Rosebud: HP; 7in (18cm); sleep eyes; no eyelashes; excellent quality doll; red dress; red striped apron; sold as a tourist doll in Copenhagen; mid 1950s.

MARKS: "Miss Rosebud" (back); "Gudrun//Formby//Danish Design// Copenhagaen Denmark (tag)

SEE: *Illustration 338. Marge Meisinger Collection.*

PRICE: $30-35

338.

Miss Rosebud (doll on right): HP; 7in (18cm); (for general characteristics, see *Illustration 337*); painted lashes above eyes; mohair wig; non-walker; had two different types of feet; dolls were often dressed in national costumes; mid 1950s.

Sarold Girl (doll on left): 7in (18cm); jointed at neck, shoulders and hips; unusual molded, painted raised eyebrows; metal arm hook (see Identification Guide, page 235); non-walker; mid 1950s.
> MARKS: "Miss Rosebud" (back);
> "Sarold" (back)
> SEE: *Illustration 339. Marge Meisinger Collection.*
> PRICE: $30-35 each

Miss Rosebud: HP; 7½in (19cm); straight-leg walker; painted eyelashes above eyes; dressed in kilt and black velvet jacket; *Ginny*®-type doll; mid 1950s.
> MARKS: "Rosebud" signed in script (head)
> SEE: *Illustration 340. Barbara Comienski Collection.*
> PRICE:$30-35

339.

340.

Société Français Fabrication
Bébé et Jouets

Like most other doll manufacturers throughout the world, S.F.B.J. began experimenting with doll molds after World War II. By 1947 they had begun to produce dolls using modern plastic material. During the early 1950s they made dolls in both rigid and flexible plastics. Their hair styles and clothes followed the latest fashions for French children. In keeping with modern clothes, these dolls often wore sportswear including slacks and bathing suits.

Girl: composition-plastic body; lighter plastic head; 15in (38cm); jointed at neck, shoulders and hips; inset eyes; lovely flesh tone on face; closed mouth; early 1950s.
  MARKS: "Jumeau" (head)
  SEE: *Illustration 341. Roslyn Nigoff Collection.*
  PRICE: $85-125+ (in original clothes)

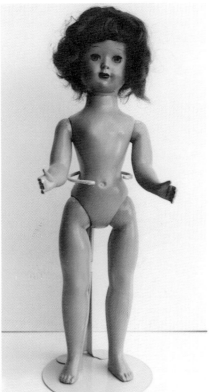

341.

Sarold (England)

The registered trademarks, the trademarks and the copyrights appearing in italics within this chapter belong to Sarold.

342.

Girl: HP; 8in (20cm); jointed at neck, shoulders and hips; no defined toes; molded raised eyebrows; metal arm hook (see Identification Guide, page 235); dolls have different faces but otherwise have same characteristics; non-walking doll; early 1950s. Sarold registered a trademark number 689831 on June 14, 1950. They made inexpensive dolls and are believed to have sold quantities of hard plastic dolls to Woolworths. (See World Wide Dolls, page 230 and Rosebud Dolls, page 198).

MARKS: "Sarold" (body)
SEE: *Illustration 342. Marge Meisinger Collection.*
PRICE: $20-30 (in original clothes)
IDENTIFICATION FEATURE:
Raised eyebrows

Sayco Doll Corporation

The registered trademarks, the trademarks and the copyrights appearing in italics within this chapter belong to Sayco Doll Corporation.

The *Miss America Pageant Doll* was made about 1959 which was later than most of the other "chubby" hard plastic type dolls. There is only one picture of her in this book but there is a large section in *Glamour Dolls of the 1950s and 1960s*, pages 203-206. There are pictures of her entire wardrobe of 50 costumes. Her wardrobe reflects the fashion changes at the end of the 1950s: (see Identification Guide, page 247 for gripper snap fastener).

MARKS: "s" (head); or "Sayco" (head); or some dolls are unmarked.

343.

Miss America Pageant Doll-Wave: HP with vinyl head; 10³/₄in (27cm); brochure says 11in (28cm); rooted hair; excellent flesh color with rosy cheeks; unusually long eyebrows; sleep eyes with molded lashes; no painted eyelashes; flat, but beautiful face; small gap between neck and head; jointed at shoulders, neck, hips and knees; arm hooks (see Identification Guide, *Hard Plastic Dolls, I*, page 268U); individual fingers; dimples above fingers but not toes; "chubby" type; original Wave uniform; metal stars on collar; red chevron on sleeve; pocketbook with USA on it; doll came with 50 outfits which could be purchased; circa 1959.

MARKS: Small "s" (head)
SEE: *Illustration 343.*
PRICE: $50-70 (including box and brochure)
$25-50 (outfits)

Dream Girl Costume: Sayco made a line of outfits called *Dream Girl* which fit all 8in (20cm) walking dolls. One of these included a pretty pink felt skirt and pink sweater set; white shoes; the inner part of the gripper snap on the skirt says, "Dot Snapper;" circa 1955-1957.

MARKS: "Dream Girl//by Sayco// Sayco Doll Corp." (box)
SEE: *Illustration 344. Pat Parton Collection.*
PRICE: $10-12

344.

Standard Doll Co.

The registered trademarks, the trademarks and the copyrights appearing in italics within this chapter belong to Standard Doll Co.

Ar-Doll Debuteens: HP; 15in (38cm); character dolls; sleep eyes; Saran hair that can be shampooed, combed, washed and curled; series includes a *Bride, Bridesmaid, Glamour Girl, Cinderella, Carmen* and *Alice in Wonderland;* unusual talking dolls with human voices; 1951.

Miniature Character Dolls: HP; 8in (20cm) sleep eyes with lashes; series includes *Brides, Bridesmaids, Dolls of all Nations* and *Famous Characters of Fact and Fiction;* 1951.

SEE: *Illustration 345. Playthings,* March 1951.
PRICE: $20-25 15in (38cm)
$10-12 8in (20cm)

345.

Stephanie Playthings, Inc.

346.

Stephanie and *Stephan:* HP; 30in (76cm); walking dolls; 1950.
>   SEE: *Illustration 346. Playthings,* June 1950.
>   PRICE: $80-90 each

Tanzpuppe-Sweetheart (Western Germany)

347.

Vatican Guard: European HP; 7in (18cm) key wind dancer; molded hair; red, yellow and purple felt uniform; black tam; circa 1960s.
>   MARKS: "Western Germany" (leg); "Tanzuppe DBGM1669844" (box)
>   SEE: *Illustration 347.*
>   PRICE: $18-25

Terri Lee, Inc.

The registered trademarks, the trademarks and the copyrights appearing in italics within this chapter belong to Terri Lee, Inc., unless otherwise noted.

Terri Lee and Jerri Welcome a New Baby Sister: HP; 16in (41cm); glued-on wig of various colors; distinctive features and eyes which are painted; very heavy doll; many clothes available that were all well made; red dots painted in nose like old china dolls; thicker lips than the *Mary Jane*® which is a *Terri Lee* look-alike; four fingers molded together with separate thumb; single line on seat. *Linda Lee* is an all-vinyl doll; 1951.

> MARKS: Early doll "Terri Lee, Pat. Pending;" later doll marked "Terri Lee"
> SEE: *Illustration 348. Playthings,* March 1951.
> PRICE: $200-250 (dolls with special outfits may be much higher)

Terri Lee and Jerry Welcome A New Baby Sister
LINDA LEE

Gene Autry: HP; 16in (41cm); (see general characteristics for *Terri Lee* dolls, *Illustration 348*); face painted differently; original red checked shirt; blue jeans; brown belt; 1947.

> MARKS: "Terri Lee, Pat. Pending" (body)
> SEE: *Illustration 349. Kathy George Collection.*
> PRICE: $500-600 (very few sample prices available)

Benjie: HP; 16in (41cm); (see general characteristics for *Terri Lee* dolls, Illustration 348); lamb's wool wig; white sweater top with red trim; red short pants; red and white socks; white hat; 1952.

> MARKS: "Terri Lee" (back)
> SEE: *Illustration 350. Kathy George Collection.*
> PRICE: $350-450 (very few sample prices available)

348.

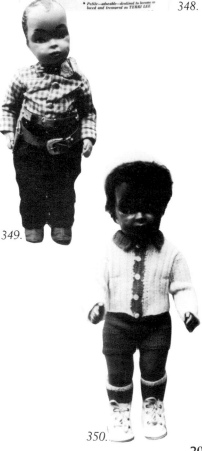

349.

350.

Mary Jane® is a registered trademark of G., H. and E. Freydberg, Inc.

Southern Belle: HP; 16in (41cm); (for general characteristics, see page   ); catalog description of outfit says, "Here I am, a true Southern Belle in taffeta dress, trimmed in narrow black velvet ribbon. I wear a rosebud chintz apron and large bow in my curls. My full petticoat and long pantaloons are eyelet trimmed. Whenever I wear this costume, Jerri pretends he's a gallant gentleman from the deep South."

MARKS: "Terri Lee, Pat. Pending" (back)

SEE: *Illustration 351* (Color Section, page 217).

PRICE: $275-300

A Day in the Life of Terri Lee: HP; (for general characteristics see, *Illustration 348*); E. toe dancing costume of silver lamé and nylon tulle; silver kid toe slippers; F. official Brownie uniform; G. gay squaw skirt and white blouse in cotton; H. percale playdress in assorted colors; J. silver lamé evening coat with taffeta lining, formal gown of nylon tulle, satin and taffeta in pastels, silver slippers; K. lounging pajamas, housecoat, felt Elly Elf slippers; L. nylon can-can slip and panties; 1951.

D. *Baby Linda* is all vinyl. A layette, playpen and wardrobe trunk could be purchased separately.

SEE: *Illustration 352.* May Company, Cleveland, Ohio, Christmas catalog, 1951.

352.

Tiny Terri and Tiny Jerri: HP; 10in (25cm); glued-on wigs; *Jerry* has a fur wig; sleep eyes; head-turning walker; painted features that are identified with *Terri Lee*; 1st, 2nd and 3rd, fingers molded together; red and blue checked matching shirts and blue jeans; circa 1956.

MARKS: "C" (back in circle)

SEE: *Illustration 353* (Color Section, page 218).

PRICE: $135-150 (*Tiny Terri Lee*)

$170-185 (*Tiny Jerri Lee*)

206

Terri Lee Get in the Swim: HP; (for general characteristics see, page 205); beach bag and swim kit complete with beach sandals, beach towel, sunglasses, sunsuit, bandana, beach coat, swimsuit, and life saver; 1953.
  SEE: *Illustration 354. Playthings,* June 1953.

Jerri Lee, Tiny Jerri, Connie Lynn, Tiny Terri, Terri Lee; Baby Linda: matching outfits; cotton clothes with striped trim in various colors; 1957.
  SEE: *Illustration 355. Toys and Novelties,* February 1957.

354.   355.

Togs and Dolls Corp.

356.

Mary Jane: HP body and vinyl head; unusual large sleep eyes with lashes; golden brown hair; jointed at neck, arms and legs; head-turning walker; 2nd and 3rd fingers molded together; dimples below fingers and on knees; all original; pink checked dress with white lace and black ribbon and rickrack trim; black leather shoes; circa 1955-1957.
  MARKS: None (doll); "My name is Mary Jane//I am made of Celanese acetate plastic//I have 36 pretty outfits//Do you have them all?" (tag)
  SEE: *Illustration 356.*
  PRICE: $75-100

207

Uneeda Doll Company, Inc.

Needa Toddles: HP head; vinyl arms and legs which are wired on; composition body; 22in (56cm); open mouth with two teeth; dimples on knees; walking apparatus advertised as "Magic Muscle;" Saran wig with curly hair; 1951.

A 1952 advertisement gives the height as 23in (58cm). The doll pictured has long braids.

MARKS: Some dolls have a "20" on head

SEE: *Illustration 357. Playthings*, September 1951.

PRICE: $65-85

Magic Fairy Princess Doll: HP body with vinyl head; 18in (46cm); pink rooted hair; jointed at neck, shoulders, hips and knees; sleep eyes; original fairy costume; white satin top; white net tutu with glitter; plastic wings; silver slippers; circa 1957.

MARKS: "Uneeda" (head); "210" (body); "The//Magic//Fairy//Princess Doll// Walks, Sits, Bends//Her Knees//Rooted//Washable Hair//by Uneeda" (tag)

SEE: *Illustration 358. Roslyn Nigoff Collection.*

PRICE: $50-70

357.

358.

Unica (Belgium)

The Unica Company was founded in 1921 and made many beautiful and innovative dolls. By 1940 it had become one of the most important manufacturers in Europe, employing up to 400 people and using the most advanced techniques.

Its premises were destroyed during World War II but by 1950 it again had become a prominent manufacturer. In the early 1960s its activities slacked down because it had failed to understand the growing demand for cheaper items. It did not cope with the ever-growing competition of cheap labor from the Orient.

In 1971 a fire completely destroyed the manufacturing facilities, archives, and so forth. The owners decided not to reconstruct the plant and converted their activities to wholesaling of general toys.

Since then they have become one of the leading toy importers and distributors in Belgium. The dolls made by Unica, especially in the periods 1930-1939 and 1947-1965, are much in demand by collectors but very few seem to be left.

The above information came from J. Libeer, Managing Director of the present Unica Company.

Many of the dolls have a deep tan skin tone and they are very beautiful and cleverly designed. They are usually well marked, often with a crown of some type. Like many of the hard plastic dolls made outside of the United States, the hard plastic doll in *Illustration 359* has a cryer placed inside.

Blonde Rooted Hair Doll: European HP; 14in (36cm); head covered with unusual rubber cap holding rooted blonde hair which is glued to head; cap can be seen in photograph; brilliant blue sleep eyes with lashes; 2nd and 3rd fingers molded together; cryer inside body; clothes not original; circa 1955-1958.

> MARKS: "UNICA//(Picture of Crown)//Belgium" (back)
> SEE: *Illustration 359. Private Collection.*
> PRICE: $35-50

359.

Valentine Dolls, Inc.

The registered trademarks, the trademarks and the copyrights appearing in italics within this chapter belong to Valentine Dolls, Inc.

Mona Lisa: HP; 12in (31cm); painted lashes under sleep eyes; jointed at neck, arms and hips; molded P.M.A. shoes under regular shoes (see *Hard Plastic Dolls, I,* Identification Guide, page 283A); unusually flat arms; doll came with wardrobe in trunk; original dress with yellow piqué skirt and sleeves, white top and trim; other clothes include a blue striped taffeta dress and pants with lace trim; red cotton print bathing suit with white and navy print towel; blue plastic bathing hat; extra shoes and socks; two curlers on card; circa mid 1950s.

> MARKS: "Your new Mona Lisa Doll has Saran hair that can be washed-combed-waved-curled"; (tag); none (doll)
> SEE: *Illustration 360* (Color Section, page 223). *Pat Parton Collection.*
> PRICE: $60-80

Ballerina Dolls: HP with vinyl head; height unknown; initial offering by company of a ballerina doll that was jointed at the knee and ankle; shoes by Capezio.

Dressmaker Doll: HP; sewing form came with doll; no patterns needed; trimmings and basic materials and sleeve board included; brochure explained the few simple steps to follow.

> MARKS: Not given in advertisement but these dolls often had "VW" and a number on their heads
> SEE: *Illustration 361. Playthings,* April 1955.
> PRICE: $45-65 each

361.

Virga Doll Company

The Beehler Arts Company had several divisions of their company which sold many different lines of dolls. As early as August 1949 they advertised their 5in (13cm) Virga Doll series in *Playthings*.

In the mid 1950s their various divisions made *Ginny*® look-alikes that were called *Lucy, GoGo, Lolly Pop, Play-mates, Play-Pals, Kim*®, *Pam*®, *Ninette*® and *Starlet Lustercreme Shampoo Doll*®, and others. The quality of their dolls was uneven and they offered dolls in most price ranges. Each year they presented a new line of dolls, clothes and accessories which were colorful and appealed to children.

For the most part, the *Ginny*®-type dolls had the same body characteristics but like most of the doll companies of the 1950s, they purchased from the manufacturers of doll parts and often took what was available. The list of doll characteristics given on page 112 of the Fortune chapter applies to the majority of the Beehler Arts dolls.

Virga Doll Series: HP; 5in (13cm); 12 in series; dolls wear pastel dresses which illustrate nursery rhymes; five have colorful party dresses; the bridal party consists of a bride, maid-of-honor and bridesmaid; jointed at neck, shoulders and hips; facial coloring and shoes have special lacquer paint; 1949.

Beehler Arts was one of the first companies to sell hard plastic dolls. Their extensive Virga line was popular for many years.

Illustrated are 1. a nursery rhyme doll; 2. a party doll with a feather on her hat; 3. bride.

   MARKS: None (doll)
   SEE: *Illustration 362. Playthings*, August 1949.

The party doll, the bride and the nursery-rhyme doll are representative of the Five-Inch Virga Doll series in which each doll is patterned after the same mold.

142

362.

Lolly-Pop Walking Doll: HP; 8in (20cm); head-turning walker; Fortune *Pam*® characteristics except for arm hook; standard arm hook (see Identification Guide, *Hard Plastic Dolls, I*, page 265K); molded-on slippers (see Identification Guide, *Illustration 431*); purple rayon embossed dress with white nylon trim; purple wig, all original clothes; mid 1950s.

Poem on box: A Virga Doll for little girls.
> Has hair that washes, also curls.
> A Virga doll to dress and play,
> The perfect doll to share your day.

MARKS: None on doll; "Virga//play//mates//LOLLY-POP//WALKING DOLL" (box)

SEE: *Illustration 363* (Color Section, page 219).

PRICE: $50-80 + (in box)

Playmate in Jodhpurs: HP; 8in (20cm); head-turning walker; for general characteristics, see Fortune section, page 112; all original; red jodhpurs; red flannel jacket and hat; black boots; mid 1950s.

The *Kim*® doll on page 141 has the same riding outfit as the Virga doll. Both dolls were made by the same company and marketed under a different name.

MARKS: None (body); "Virga//play//mates//WALKING DOLL//Riding Habit 198" (box)

SEE: *Illustration 364.*

PRICE: $50-80 +

364.

Schiaparelli GoGo Skater: HP; 8in (20cm); (see page 112 for general characteristics); of Fortune-Virga and other Beehler Arts dolls.

Madame Schiaparelli, the French clothes designer of the 1950s, designed a line of beautiful clothes for the Virga Company (see *Hard Plastic Dolls, I*, page 241 and *Glamour Dolls of the 1950s and 1960s*, page 220 for more information).

MARKS: None (doll); "Schiaparelli" (tag sewn into dress)

SEE: *Illustration 365. Nancy Carlton Collection.*

PRICE: $85-100 (more for exceptional costumes)

Kim® is a registered trademark of Kim Doll Co.
Pam® is a registered trademark of Fortune Toys, Inc.   365.

Lucy: HP; 9in (23cm); blonde wig; sleep eyes with molded lashes; high arched eyebrow; head-turning walker; standard arm hooks; jointed at neck, shoulders and hips; individual fingers; dimples above each finger; two dimples on each knee; excellent toe detail; no dimples above toes; boxed clothes include a white piqué dress with red polka dot top and cape; blue polka dot plastic rain cape; green felt jacket, shoes, stockings, and so forth; circa 1955.

> **MARKS:** None (doll); "My Name Is Lucy 'I walk'//by Virga" (printed on inside of box)
> **SEE:** *Illustration 366. Marge Meisinger Collection.*
> **PRICE:** $50-80 (in box)

366.

Play-Pals Walking Doll: HP; 9in (23cm); pin-jointed head-turning walker; sleep eyes; molded lashes; blonde mohair wig; pointed painted eyebrows; individual fingers; dots over fingers; no dots over toes; deep impression under nose; beautiful flesh tone with rosy cheeks; two dimples on each knee; wardrobe includes white and pink dress trimmed with lace; pink robe with blue bias trim; yellow pajamas with pink bias trim; inside part of gripper snap says "RAU SKLIKITS;" circa mid 1950s.

> **MARKS:** None (doll); "Virga Play-Pals//Walking Doll//Manufactured by Beehler Arts Ltd." (box)
> **SEE:** *Illustration 367. Pat Parton Collection.*
> **PRICE:** $50-80 (in box)

367.

Hi Heel 'Teen:

This doll was an inexpensive doll which competed with the "glamour" high-heeled dolls which were popular about 1957-1965. The Beehler Arts Company had several marketing companies which sold these dolls using similar boxes, but colored differently. The dolls had several different names including *Kim*®. They had fashionable but inexpensive clothes. The thin jointed legs are an identification feature (see Identification Guide, page 242).

    MARKS: None (doll); boxes marked with the name of the marketing company of the doll.

Hi-Heel 'Teen: HP; 8½in (22cm); sleep eyes with painted eyelashes above eyes; platinum hair; excellent flesh color; jointed at neck, arms, legs and above knees; high-heeled feet; 2nd and 3rd fingers molded together and curved toward hand; sharp mold lines on arms and legs; unusually thin legs (see Identification Guide, page 242); standard arm hooks (see Identification Guide, *Hard Plastic Dolls, I*, page 265); head-turning walker; flannel dress with black top trimmed with lace and print skirt; black pillbox-type hat with large red rose; all original; circa 1956-1957. It competed with the Alexander *Cissette*®. (See also *Kim*® dolls, page 140).

    MARKS: None (doll); "Beautiful Virga Dolls//Hi-Heel 'Teen//manufactured by Beehler Arts Ltd.//H-H 3" (box)

368.

SEE: *Illustration 368.*
PRICE: $20-25

Hi Heel 'Teen: HP; 8½in (22cm); same characteristics as the other *Hi Heel 'Teen, Illustration 368*; blue taffeta dress and blue net overskirt with glitter; pink high-heel shoes; all original; circa 1956-1957.

    MARKS: None (doll); "Beautiful Virga Dolls//Hi-Heel 'Teen//manufactured by Beehler Arts//H-H 3" (box)
SEE: *Illustration 369. Pat Parton Collection.*
PRICE: $20-25

369.

Vogue Dolls, Inc.

Mrs. Jennie Graves, the founder of the Vogue Doll Company, experimented with different materials and types of dolls from 1922 until 1947-1948. With the advent of hard plastic, she changed the material of her composition *Toddles* dolls to hard plastic and continued their popular size and styles. Her first 1948-1949 dolls in the new material look very much like *Toddles*.

She also experimented with a variety of names. The beloved name *Ginny* did not appear until 1952. Other early post-war dolls were *Crib Crowd, Far-Away Lands, Story Book Characters, Sister-Brother Sets* and many others.

This book features some beautiful examples of these early dolls.

Mother and Daughter: HP; 14in (36cm) and 8in (20cm); unusual advertisement for dolls with matching outfits; *Mother* doll similar to a composition doll made about 1943; the composition doll was unmarked; 1949.
The dolls in the photograph on the right were not advertised as *Ginny*. They were just 8in (20cm) dolls with "Sunday Best" clothes.
SEE: *Illustration 370. Playthings,* August 1949.

Painted-Eye Ginny Twins: HP; 8in (20cm); mohair wigs; girl dressed in pink skirt and sweater set; boy dressed in matching pink pants and sweater set; both have stockinette caps; all original; 1948-1950.
MARKS: "Vogue" (head); "Vogue" (body)
SEE: *Illustration 371* (Color Section, page 221). *Sandra Strater Collection.*
PRICE: $275-350 each (depending on outfit)

Cinderella, Prince and Fairy Godmother: HP; 8in (20cm); painted eye; strung; non-walking; 1949. (upper right in advertisement). **PRICE:** $275-350 each
Crib Crowd: HP; 8in (20cm); painted eyes; strung; non-walking; babies; 1949. (center left in advertisement) These dolls were advertised as "miniature mites with curly foundation wigs." **PRICE:** $500-550 each
Vogue Velva Wetting Baby: All HP fittings; 15in (38cm); filled with 100% foam rubber; made and tested in the laboratories of the Fuller Brush Company; will not pull apart under 65 pounds pressure; 1949 (bottom left in advertisement)
SEE: *Illustration 372. Playthings,* September 1949.

370.

372.

Fluffy: HP; 8in (20cm); marked "Fluffy" on box; sleep eyes with painted lashes above the eyes; straight legs; "Poodle" hair; green "poodle" suit; pink and green ears; non-walking; circa 1950.

> **MARKS:** "Vogue" (head); "Vogue" (body)
> **SEE:** *Illustration 373. Pat Timmons Collection.*

PRICE: $500-600+

Ginny Cowboy and Cowgirl: HP; 8in (20cm); strung non-walker; sleep eyes with painted eyelashes; girl's eyes are brown; the boy's eyes are blue; both have brown mohair wigs; both wear red felt hats; green center snap shoes; green belts with tiny metal guns; both have plaid shirts; girl has cream-colored leather-type skirt with multi-colored trim at bottom; matching vest is trimmed in red rickrack; boy has same vest; pants are cream-colored felt in back with the front made to look like chaps made of sheepskin; 1951.

> **MARKS:** "Vogue Doll" (back)
> **SEE:** *Illustration 374. Athena Crowley Collection.*

PRICE: $300-350 each

Toddler: HP; 8in (20cm); non-walker; strung; sleep eyes with painted lashes above eyes; straight legs; pink satin print dress; matching panties; pink straw hat with cloth daisies; pink shoes; blue socks; circa 1951-1952.

> **MARKS:** "Vogue" (head); "Vogue" (body)
> **SEE:** *Illustration 375. Nancy Roeder Collection.*

PRICE: $275-325

373.

374.

375.

Black Ginny: HP; 8in (20cm); sleep eyes with painted lashes; early non-walker; straight legs; pink dress with blue trim; 1952. A walker was made later.

    MARKS: "Vogue" (head); "Vogue" (body)

    SEE: *Illustration 376. Marge Meisinger Collection.*

    PRICE: $700 up (very few sample prices)

Painted Eyelash Ginny: HP; 8in (20cm); blonde poodle cut wig; sleep eyes with painted eyelashes above eyes; green felt coat with red rickrack trim; green checked dress; red ribbon in hair; all original; circa 1952.

    MARKS: "Vogue" (head); "Vogue" (body)

    SEE: *Illustration 377. Marianne Gardner Collection.*

    PRICE: $250-300

376.

Ginny Roller Skater: HP; 8in (20cm); blonde poodle cut wig; sleep eyes with painted eyelashes above eyes; red and white skating costume; red snap shoes with skates; excellent condition with good color; 1952.

    SEE: *Illustration 378. Marianne Gardner Collection.*

    PRICE: $250-350

377.

378.

Continued on page 225.

Terri Lee *Southern Belle* (see page 206).

Terri Lee *Tiny Jerri* and *Tiny Terri* (see page 206).

Virga *Playmate Lolly-Pop* (see page 211).

Richwood *Sandra Sue* (see page 190).

Vogue painted-eye *Ginny Twins* (see page 214). *Sandra Strater Collection.*

Nancy Ann *Roy Rogers* and *Dale Evans* (see page 157). *Nancy Catlin Collection.*

221

Vogue *Ginny Cowgirls* and *Cowboy* (see page 227). *Marge Meisinger Collection.*

Vogue *Ginny in Trunk* (see page 225). *Dorothy Hesner Collection.*

Lenci (Italy) provincial
dolls (see page 144).

223

Reliable (Canada) *Plassikins* (see page 188).

Bible Doll Co. of America *David* (see page 68). *Eunice Kier Collection.*

Continued from page 216.

Ginny Skater from Sports Series: HP; 8in (20cm); sleep eyes with painted eyelashes; green felt top; pink felt skirt with felt applique; ice skates; mint condition with excellent color; 1952.

> **SEE:** *Illustration 379. Marianne Gardner Collection.*
>
> **PRICE:** $250-300+

Ginny: HP; 8in (20cm); head-turning walker; sleep eyes; came in double fold cardboard travel case; wardrobe includes party dress, straw hat, nightgown, robe, playsuit, towel, slippers, mirror, comb, garden tools, panties, shoes and shampoo cape; 1954. This is the year *Ginny* became a walker.

> **SEE:** *Illustration 380.* Marshall Field & Co. Christmas catalog, 1954. *Barbara Andresen Collection.*
>
> **PRICE:** $400-500 up (very few sample prices available)

Ginny in Trunk with Clothes: HP; 8in (20cm); non-walker; sleep eyes with painted lashes above eyes; straight legs; panties and cape on doll; right side of box has white kimono with red dots, nightgown curlers, booties and soft plastic shoes; left side of box has yellow organdy dress (tagged), straw hat with blue flowers and an extra pair of shoes with ties in center; doll wears sunglasses; circa 1953. The trunk is cardboard with country and steamship labels. It also has a "Dolly Airlines" label.

> **MARKS:** "Ginny//My Beautiful Real-Looking Hair Can Be//Wet, Combed, Curled & Set" (tag); "Vogue Dolls" (dress tag)
>
> **SEE:** *Illustration 381.* (Color Section, page 222). *Dorothy Hesner Collection.*
>
> **PRICE:** $400-500 up (very few prices available)

379.

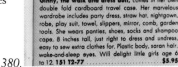

Ginny, the walk and dress doll, comes in her own double fold cardboard travel case. Her marvelous wardrobe includes party dress, straw hat, nightgown, robe, play suit, towel, slippers, mirror, comb, garden tools. She wears panties, shoes, socks and shampoo cape. 8 inches tall, just right to dress and undress, easy to sew extra clothes for. Plastic body, saran hair, wake-and-sleep eyes. Will delight little girls age 6 to 12. **151 T2-77** **$5.95**

380.

Ginny: HP; 8in (20cm); dressed in Easter coat and straw hat; purse with "Ginny" printed on it; *Ginny's* pup made by Steiff; 1955.

SEE: *Illustration 382. Playthings,* April 1955.

Ginny: HP; 8in (20cm); straight leg walker; advertisement from 1955 Christmas toy catalog of The May Company in Cleveland, Ohio.
Clothes top row from left to right: 1. gray organdy dress with pink trim 2. checked overalls with yellow jersey and brown cap 3. blue dress with black straw hat 4. cowgirl outfit 5. blue and white Dutch girl outfit. Clothes bottom row from left to right: 1. red dress 2. roller skater 3. bride 4. velvet coat, fur muff and beret.
Ginny's baby sister, *Ginette:* soft vinyl; 8in (20cm)

SEE: *Illustration 383.*

382.

383.

Ginny Cowgirls and Cowboy: HP; 8in (20cm); different cowboy and cowgirl outfits made by Vogue.
Left to right:
1. Purple felt skirt with gold trim; chartreuse top with rickrack trim; fuchsia vest with gold trim; purple felt cowboy hat; fuchsia boots; carrying a gold gun; Vogue label on dress. *Marge Meisinger Collection.*
2. Green felt skirt with print of horse; red blouse; chartreuse vest with print of steer; carrying a gold gun; Vogue label on dress.
3. Cowboy doll with short blonde hair; green felt cowboy pants with print of horses; red top; chartreuse cowboy hat; carrying a gold gun; Vogue label on suit. *Marge Meisinger Collection.*
4. Blue cowgirl dress with silver black cotton trim at neck and sleeves; silver fringe braid; black leather belt; white holster with silver gun which is molded like the gold guns; Vogue label on dress. *Marge Meisinger Collection.*

SEE: *Illustration 384* (Color Section, page 222).

385.

Ginny: HP; 8in (20cm); bent-knee walker; plastic molded eyelashes; red bathing suit with "Ginny" knit into material; circa 1957-1962.

MARKS: "Vogue" (head); "Ginny Vogue Dolls, Inc. Pat #2687594 Made in U.S.A." (body)
SEE: *Illustration 385.*
PRICE: $125-150

Ginny from Far-Away Lands: HP; 8in (20cm); bent-knee late *Ginny*; series included:
1. *Highlander* 2. *Scandinavian* 3. *Hollander* 4. *Hawaiian* 5. *Oriental* 6. *Israelian* 7. *Alaskan*; 1959.

SEE: *Illustration 386. Playthings*, March 1959.

386.

Here's Ginny in seven costume wonders of the world! Colorful Highlander costume representing the *British Isles* . . . native *Scandinavian* costume . . . delightful little *Hollander* costume . . . exotic *Hawaiian* costume . . . traditional *Oriental* costume . . . an *Israelian* costume from the Near East . . . even a dramatic *Alaskan* costume in honor of our 49th state!

A World of Promotion for You! Here's new excitement — new drama — and additional sales for you. This idea is perfect for tie-in promotion — newspaper ads . . . window displays . . . counter set-ups. These new costumes are sales-appealing in every way — and every little girl is a prospect because it's Ginny! Display them for sure and you'll sell them — *for sure!*

Girl in Pink: painted HP; 14½in (37cm); lovely wig with hair braided and roller at sides; sleep eyes; painted eyelashes under eyes; closed mouth; early standard arm hook (see Identification Guide, *Hard Plastic Dolls, I,* page 262A); unusually slender body with long legs; all original clothes; pink organdy dress and teddy; pink cotton slip attached to skirt; pink leather buckle shoes; 1st, 2nd and 3rd fingers molded together with the little finger only molded part way; Vogue clothing characteristics; lace trim ⬱ on dress; circa 1949.

> MARKS: "14" (head); "Made in U.S.A." (body). There is no circle around mark. "Vogue Dolls" (tag sewn into dress)

> SEE: *Illustration 387. Shirley Niziolek Collection.*

> PRICE: (rare doll — very few sample prices)

387.

Littlest Angel: HP body with vinyl head; 11in (28cm); sleep eyes; straight rooted hair; walker; jointed at neck, shoulders, hips and knees; 1962.

This is from a 1962 Vogue brochure. The *Littlest Angel* is no longer advertised under the Arranbee name. She has now become *Ginny's* cousin and part of the *Ginny* family. She likes to visit the *Ginny* family and bring her complete wardrobe with her.

Top row from left to right:
1. Basic *Little Angel* with panties, shoes and socks.
2. *Picnic Fun:* matching *Ginny* outfit with white cotton deck pants and red print overblouse.
3. *Patriotic Dress:* white piqué dress with red, white and blue trim.

Bottom row from left to right:
1. Two-piece pajamas.
2. Pink batiste dress with lace trim; satiny bow; rosebuds.
3. Blue dot cotton school dress; crisp white pinafore.
4. Red party dress with full skirt trimmed with lace.

> SEE: *Illustration 388. Brochure from the Kathryn Davis Collection.* (See illustrations in Arranbee section of this book. See also the illustrations in *Glamour Dolls of the 1950s and 1960s* under Arranbee.)

388.

Jill: HP; 10in (25cm); sleep eyes with molded lashes; pierced ears; jointed knees; high-heeled feet; painted fingernails; adult figure; arm hook similar to *Ginny.*

Jill was introduced at the Toy Fair in New York in February 1957. The March issue of *Playthings* featured a beautiful pop-up section of the Vogue dolls. This lovely version of *Jill* with the beautiful background folded out of the magazine.

MARKS: "Vogue" (head); "Jill/Vogue, Made in USA, 1957" (body)

SEE: *Illustration 389. Playthings,* March 1957. (See inside title page for photograph.)

PRICE: $75-100 (depending on outfit)

Jill: HP; 10in (25cm); sleep eyes with molded lashes; pierced ears; jointed knees; high-heeled feet; painted fingernails; adult figure; armhole hook similar to *Ginny;* (for *Jill* clothes brochure, see *Hard Plastic Dolls, I,* pages 251-255).

MARKS: "Vogue" (head); "Jill// Vogue, Made in USA, 1957" (body)

SEE: *Illustration 390. Lois Janner Collection.*

PRICE: $85-110 (depending on outfit)

390.

Walkalon Mfg. Company

The registered trademarks, the trademarks and the copyrights appearing in italics within this chapter belong to Walkalon Mfg. Company.

Betsy Walker: HP head; tenite body; 21in (53cm); early key-winding walking doll which walks alone and swings her arms, legs and head; pink organdy dress with Koroseal panties; brown sleep eyes; 1950.

MARKS: None (doll); "Warren// Three Oaks (picture of 3 trees) Michigan" (tag on panties)

SEE: *Illustration 391. Playthings,* August 1950.

Betsy Walker: HP; 20in (51cm); key-winding walking doll; brown sleep eyes; still in working condition; (not shown dressed in original pink organdy dress and bonnet); (see *Illustration 391*).

MARKS: None (doll); "Warren// Three Oaks (picture of 3 trees) Michigan" (tag on panties)

SEE: *Illustration 392. Arline Last Collection.*

PRICE: $75-90 (in working condition)
$100+ (mint-in-box)

391.

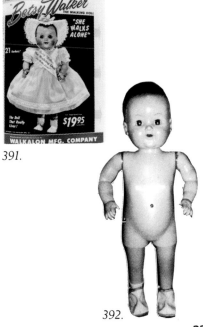

392.

World Wide Doll Club
(Overseas Dolls)

Brochure: The Nabisco Wheat Honeys and Rice Honeys offered these dolls as a premium about 1959. The brochure said, "Fabulous dolls...made patiently in little shops and peasant cottages where dollmaking is an art and a loving tradition. Dolls are dressed by artisans with the same deft touches that make their grandmothers' dolls museum pieces. Rich fabrics or home-spun types — whatever material is used is characteristic of the doll-making tradition in the country of origin.

"DOLLS ARE HISTORY IN MINIATURE

"Dolls tell you so much about the land they come from — the customs, station in life, occupation, religion or even the region of the country. And there is always some extra surprise — a coin or perhaps an extra stamp, or some other curiosity. No wonder these dolls inspire interest in history, geography and language!"

Originally these dolls cost $1.00 or $1.25 and two boxtops from Wheat Honeys or Rice Honeys. The coupon was sent to Locust Valley, L.I., N.Y. However, the dolls were mailed to the customer from the country of origin. The dolls' material and construction varied widely as did the costuming. The advertising concept is unusual.

The following dolls were offered:

1. Italy — *Zita* from Palermo and *Valentino* from Tormina.
2. Japan — *Higasa* in kimono and *Ichiro* with samaurai sword.
3. Israel — *Jessica* with pottery jar and *Aaron*, a carpet seller.
4. Korea — *Tai-Mu*, a dancer and *Bock-Dong* who beats a drum.
5. Scotland — *Meg* and *Gregory*, both in a tartan.
6. Greece — *Althea* in native costume and *Tassos* wearing uniform of the Royal Guard.
7. Malta — *Elena* wears the black faldetta and *Nardo* is a fisherman.
8. Holland — *Juliana* in Dutch dress and *Pieter* in Dutch pantaloons.
9. Portugal — *Petita* has an embroidered apron and *Fernando* is a fisherman.
10. Switzerland — *Herta* has a festival costume and *Ludwig* is an Alpine climber.
11. South Africa — *Nomsa* carries a baby on her back and *Fanou* has a spear and shield.
12. Arabia — *Mabruka* is a dancer and *Omar* is a desert sheik.

393.

Your Overseas Doll Gregory from Scotland: HP; 6½in (17cm); sleep eyes with no lashes; sculptured, molded eyebrows; jointed at neck and shoulders only; mold mark runs through sculptured ear; dressed in traditional Stuart plaid Scottish kilt; black wool jacket; white shirt with jabot; Scottish hat; molded slipper shoes which have been painted black; painted-on socks; individual fingers; plastic purse holds Scottish flag and English 1956 farthing with a picture of Queen Elizabeth; circa 1958-59. This doll was probably made by the Sarold Mfg. Co. (see page 202).

394.

MARKS: None (doll); "Nabisco Wheat Honeys or Rice Honeys Collector Dolls from around the world.!"
SEE: *Illustration 393.*
PRICE: $15-20

Heidi: HP; glass eyes; HP eyelashes; mohair wig; painted-on white socks and blue shoes; royal blue skirt; light blue apron; black vest; white blouse; straw hat with ribbons and flowers; all original in box; mailed from Zurich, Switzerland, March 20, 1958. This doll came with a letter explaining the customs and geography of Switzerland. She did not seem to be connected with the Nabisco premium set of foreign dolls but her dress was the same as *Herta* in the Nabisco set.
SEE: *Illustration 394. Carmen P. Smotherman Collection.*
PRICE: $20-30 (without box)

Writing Toys Corporation

The registered trademarks, the trademarks and the copyrights appearing in italics within this chapter belong to Writing Toys Corporation.

Manuel von Rabenau was the inventor-creator of *Rita, the Writing Doll*. He was granted a patent in July 1959 and the doll was marketed in 1962.

Within a few weeks of the patent approval Inez Robb, feature writer of United Features Syndicate, wrote a story which was printed in many newspapers including the *New York Times*. She called *Rita* a "mentally-oriented doll."

Rita's debut was at the 1962 New York Toy Fair. Soon letters of inquiry came not only from dealers in the United States but from France, Argentina, Italy, Mexico, Germany and Japan.

Rita not only could write, but she was attractive and realistic. The original *Rita* was sculptured by Agop Agapoff, well-known New York artist.

Included with the purchase of *Rita* were three word discs, each of which wrote two words — one on each side. Additional discs could be ordered from Writing Toys Corporation.

231

Rita the Writing Doll: HP with vinyl head; 26in (66cm); battery operated; came with three cams which allowed her to write six words; blue eyes; all original; purchase price in 1962 was $29.95.

    MARKS: "First Run" (back in circle); "Writing Toys, St. Paul USA 1962" (head)

    SEE: *Illustration 395* (doll holding magic slate and stylus). *Mary Elizabeth Poole Collection.*

        Illustration 396 (operating instructions). *Mary Elizabeth Poole Collection.*

    PRICE: $150-200 in operating condition (very few sample prices available)

395.

396.

Doll Marks

All of the names in *italics* appearing in the following section are protected names. The legal protections were left off for the readability of the charts and price guide.

By far the majority of the marks for hard plastic dolls were published in *Hard Plastic Dolls I*. Because this means of identification is so important, the marks are repeated and updated in this section. The other sections of the Identification Guide show new information.

NUMBERS

1.	2S	Uneeda
2.	3	Uneeda, Richwood Toys
3.	7/3	Starr
4.	9	Ideal *Lolly*
5.	11VW	Valentine
6.	12	Valentine
7.	14	Roberta, Valentine, Star, De-Sota, Arrow, Ideal Baby Possible Vogue
8.	14R	Belle, Deluxe Reading, Eegee, Natural, Rite Lee, Royal, Sayco
9.	16	Arranbee
10.	16VW	Valentine
11.	P 16	Belle
12.	17VW	Valentine, Arranbee
13.	18V	Nancy Ann
14.	18VW	Valentine
15.	20	Uneeda
16.	20HH	Belle
17.	VP23 or UP17	Ideal
18.	23ARV	Arranbee
19.	25	Uneeda
20.	31AE	Horsman
21.	32	Ideal
22.	49 R & B	Arranbee
23.	65 R & B	Arranbee
24.	74	Arrow
25.	88	Horsman
26.	V91	Ideal
27.	P90-91-92-93-94	Ideal (*Toni* Family)
28.	P90 W	Ideal
29.	128	Valentine
30.	160-170-180	Horsman
31.	170	Baby Barry Toys
32.	180	Roberta
33.	R185	Valentine
34.	190	Wilson
35.	AE 200	Belle
36.	P 200	Ideal
37.	210	Mollye, Arranbee, Uneeda, Roberta
38.	250 R & B	Arranbee
39.	450	Mollye
40.	750	Sayco
41.	AE593	Belle
42.	2252077	Ideal
43.	2675644	American Character
44.	2687594	Vogue

PAT. PENDING — Companies using this mark
1. A & H (Pats. Pending and Pat's Pend)
2. Arranbee
3. Ideal *Posie* (back of knees on roll joint)
4. Ideal
5. Plastic Molded Arts (*Miss Joan*) (Pats. Pending)
6. Pressman (Pat. Pend.)
7. Togs & Dolls
8. Terri Lee
9. Valentine (This company sometimes has both "Made in USA" and Pat. Pending" on back)
10. Virga (Pat's Pend.)

MADE IN U.S.A.

1. American Character *Alice*	6. Hardy Different Toys	11. Roberta
2. Baby Barry Toys	7. Horsman	12. Star
3. Bal	8. Ideal	13. Sayco
4. Cast	9. Imperial	14. Uneeda
5. DeSota	10. Richwood *Cindy Lou*	15. Vogue

SYMBOLS

1. ⬦➔ Arrow
2. ⊗ Mollye
3. △ *Saucy Walker*-type — Ideal Characteristics

LETTERS

1. A	Uneeda	8. E.G.	Eegee
2. A.C.	American Character	9. MK	Ideal
3. AE	American Character, Belle, Deluxe Reading, Eegee, Mary Hoyer, Nasco, New Dolly Toy Company, P. & M. Sales, Sayco, Valentine, Unique	10. P	Ideal
		11. PMA	Plastic Molded Arts
		12. R & B	Arranbee
		13. S	Eegee
		14. s	Sayco
4. Amer. Char.	American Character	15. U	Uneeda
		16. V	Ideal
5. B	Uneeda	17. V4	Effanbee
6. ©	Terri Lee	18. VP	Ideal
7. CDC	Cosmopolitan	19. W	Ideal Walker

Identification Guide
Table of Contents

Arm Hooks

Of all the methods of identifying hard plastic dolls, the characteristics of the arm hooks can be the most helpful. This is especially true of the small walking dolls. Many of the companies seem to have their own special hook even though they purchased bodies from the few doll body companies.

It is recommended that the reader refer to *Hard Plastic Dolls, I* for most of the arm hooks of the better known hard plastic dolls. The following arm hooks are in addition to those in the first book.

WARNING: The collector must be aware of the so-called "marriages" in repaired dolls. Arms seemed to be especially vulnerable in dolls that were strung, and they were often replaced with any small arm available.

A.
1. *Sarold (England) Ginny-type Doll* (bottom arm); metal ring hook.
2. *Rosebud (England) Ginny-type* (top arm: all-plastic hook.
   SEE: *Illustration 397. Marge Meisinger Collection.*

397.

B.
Ontario Plastics Paula Sue: arm hook with squared off plastic piece holding a metal ring.
   SEE: *Illustration 398. Marge Meisinger Collection.*

C.
Nancy Ann Debbie arm hook: each arm has a different hook. The Richwood *Cindy Lou* has the same arm hooks.
   SEE: *Illustration 399. Marge Meisinger Collection.*

398.

399.

D.
Block Baby Walker Arm Hook: This hook is similar to, but not the same as the Nancy Ann *Debbie* hook (see Identification Guide, *Hard Plastic Dolls, I,* page 268U) and the Arranbee *Littlest Angel* and Vogue *Li'l Imp* (see Identification Guide, *Hard Plastic Dolls, I,* page 269Y). This hook is on both the hard plastic head and the vinyl head models.
 SEE: *Illustration 400.*

E.
(from left to right)
Arm Hooks:
1. Plastic Molded Arts *Miss Joan.*
2. Cosmopolitan jointed-arm *Ginger.*
3. Midwestern *Mary Jean.*
 SEE: *Illustration 401.*

F.
Richwood Cindy Lou Arm Hook: similar to Plastic Molded Arts arm hook in *Hard Plastic Dolls, I,* page 265M.
 SEE: *Illustration 402. Marge Meisinger Collection.*

G.
Plastic Molded Arts (PMA) Chubby-Type Doll: unusual arm hook.
 SEE: *Illustration 403. Helen M. Keefe Collection.*

400.

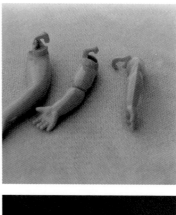

401.

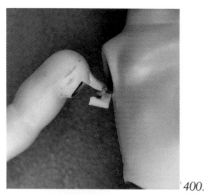

402.

403.

Bodies of 6in (15cm) to 8in (20cm) Ginny-Type Dolls

There was a gradual change in the bodies of the popular small *Ginny*-type dolls. They generally were introduced as non-walker dolls. Then the walking mechanism was added. About 1955 many of the companies added jointed knees.

About the same time, most of the companies started to make both the all-hard plastic doll and the vinyl-headed doll with rooted hair. In general, the vinyl-headed doll cost a little more money but was so popular that the all-hard plastic doll was dropped from the line. Today's collectors prefer the all-hard plastic doll, and it is interesting to note that many more of these dolls seem to have survived. The dedicated collector often finds that it is difficult to locate specific dolls with vinyl heads.

A. (left to right)
1. *A & H. Gigi:* HP; early hip-pin straight-leg walker with original box.
   SEE: *Illustration 404. Kim R. Lusk Collection.*
2. *A & H. Gigi:* HP; bent-knee walker
   SEE: *Illustration 405.*
3. *A & H. Gigi:* HP with vinyl head (not pictured); see *Illustration 14.*

B.
Allison Bonita (left) and American Character Betsy McCall (right): slim walking dolls; *Bonita* has soft vinyl head; *Betsy* has HP head.
   SEE: *Illustration 406. Marge Meisinger Collection.*

404.

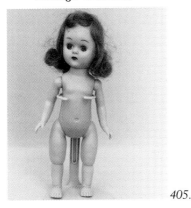

405.

406.

C.

Ginger and Ginger-Type All-HP Bodies: Left to right: 1. Midwestern *Mary Jean*, 8in (20cm) 2. Cosmopolitan *Ginger*, 7½in (19cm) with medium eyes 3. Cosmopolitan *Ginger*, 7½in (19cm) with small eyes.

Mary Jean has the same body characteristics as *Ginger* except for painted feet, an extra 1/2in (1.3cm) in height and a similar but slightly different arm hook (see Identification Guide, page 236). The other two dolls have the standard *Ginger* arm hook (see Identification Guide, *Hard Plastic Dolls, I*, page 266N).

Other *Ginger* characteristics include a mold seam through the middle ear making the center part of the ear higher than the top and the lobe; closed mouth; very faint navel; dimple under the lip that is distinctive; toes all the same length; dots above the toes; some have jointed knees with a crease in front of the ankle; a few have jointed arms (see *Illustration 150*); individual fingers; mold flaw at wrist on palm side; fingernails and joint details are excellent; all are head-turning walkers; glued-on wig; distinctive heel (see *Illustration 251*).

MARKS: None
SEE: *Illustration 407.*

407.

Five of the six *Ginger*-type dolls are shown in *Illustration 408*. The sixth *Ginger* doll is the first doll on the left in *Illustration 409*.

D.

Ginger Bodies: from left to right:

1. Early straight leg with painted eyelashes.
2. Most popular straight-leg *Ginger*; see *Illustration 421* for three variations in eyes.
3. Late bent-knee doll with bent elbows.
4. Vinyl head on hard plastic body.
5. Vinyl head on hard plastic body: Cha-Cha heel.

SEE *Illustration 408. Pat Parton Collection* (first doll on left).

408.

(Left to right) all-HP:

Cosmopolitan Ginger #6: bent knees with straight arms; head-turning walker. *Pat Parton Collection.*

E.

Richwood Sandra Sue: high heels and toe detail; walking mechanism but head does not turn (2nd doll from left).

Richwood Sandra Sue: flat feet and no toe detail; walking mechanism but head does not turn (3rd doll from left).

Roberta Walker, Doll Bodies Mary Lou, Grant Plastics Suzie: painted, molded shoes; non-walker (4th doll from left).

For general characteristics, see the company listings in this book and in *Hard Plastics Dolls, I.*

MARKS: None (dolls)
SEE: *Illustration 409.*

F.

Elite Vicki: Pam facial characteristics and arm hook; dimples above toes which have excellent detail; (this is very different from the *Pam* and *Lucy* doll which have molded slippers); jointed at neck, shoulders hips and knees; two creases at ankles.

MARKS: None (doll); "Elite Creations" (brochure)
SEE: *Illustration 410. Ester Borgis Collection.*

409.

410.

239

411.

G.

Nancy Ann Muffie (from left to right) #1: HP; straight-leg non-walker; jointed at shoulders, neck and hips; flip Dynel wig with side part; painted eyelashes above eyes; no eyebrows above eyes; molded eyelashes; straight line on seat; 1953.

    MARKS: "STORY BOOK//DOLLS//CALIFORNIA" (back)
    SEE: *Illustration 411.*

Muffie (from left to right) #2: HP; rare straight-leg non-walker; slightly different body and legs; Y on seat; a line below and above front knees; two dimples between knee lines; Dynel flip wig with side part; shorter neck than other dolls; molded eyelashes on sleep eyes; painted eyelashes and eyebrows above eyes; date unknown.

    MARKS: None (doll)
    SEE: *Illustration 411. Mary Ann Watkins Collection.*

Muffie (from left to right) #3: HP; straight-leg walker; Dynel wig in flip style with side part; wig also came in pigtails; molded eyelashes on sleep eyes; painted eyelashes above eyes; no eyebrows; head-turning walker; one straight line on seat; 1954.

    MARKS: "STORY BOOK//DOLLS//CALIFORNIA" (back)
    SEE: *Illustration 411. Mary Ann Watkins Collection.*

Muffie (from left to right) #4: HP; rare unplayed-with doll in box marked "Lori-Ann" (see *Hard Plastic Dolls, I,* page 192); came with a flocked hair twin brother in a second marked "Lori-Ann" box; girl has unusual wig with bangs and two rows of rolled curls held with hairpins; straight-leg head-turning walker; eyelashes and eyebrows above eyes; one straight line on seat; date unknown.

    MARKS: None (doll); "Lori-Ann" (box)
    SEE: *Illustration 411.*

Muffie (from left to right) #5: HP; straight-leg head-turning walker; molded lashes on sleep eyes; eyelashes and eyebrows painted above eyes; one line on seat; circa 1954-56.

    MARKS: "STORY BOOK//DOLLS//CALIFORNIA//MUFFIE" (back)
    SEE: *Illustration 411. Mary Ann Watkins Collection.*

Muffie (from left to right) #6: HP; same as #5 except that it is a bent-knee head-turning walker; painted eyebrows and eyelashes above eyes; one straight line on seat; circa 1954-1956.

  MARKS: "STORY BOOK//DOLLS// CALIFORNIA//MUFFIE" (back)

  SEE: *Illustration 412. Mary Ann Watkins Collection.*

Muffie (from left to right) #7: HP with vinyl head; bent-knee head-turning walker; painted eyelashes and eyebrows above eyes; molded eyelashes on sleep eyes; one line on seat; 1956+.

  MARKS: "STORY BOOK//DOLLS// CALIFORNIA//MUFFIE" (back); large "NANCY ANN" (head)

  SEE: *Illustration 412.*

Muffie (from left to right) #8: HP with vinyl head; head-turning walker; same doll as #7 except for straight legs; rooted ponytail; 1956+.

  MARKS: "STORY BOOK//DOLLS// CALIFORNIA//MUFFIE" (back); "Nancy Ann" (in small letters on back of head)

  SEE: *Illustration 412.*

412.

413.

Muffie (from left to right) #9: HP; plastic walking mechanism; head-turning walker; beautiful, but slightly different skin tone; heavier wide-set legs; eyelashes painted below eyes; plastic eyelashes over sleep eyes; 1967.

  SEE: *Illustration 413.*

H.
Ontario Plastics Paula Sue: early non-walking *Ginny*-type.

  SEE: *Illustration 414. Marge Meisinger Collection.*

414.

I. (from left to right)
1. *Uneeda:* HP body and vinyl head.
2. *Hollywood:* all-HP.
3. *Allison:* HP body and vinyl head.
4. *Plastic Molded Arts:* HP body and vinyl head.
SEE: *Illustration 415. Marge Meisinger Collection.*

J.
High-Heel 'Teen: HP; slender figure; jointed at neck, shoulders, hips and knees.
MARKS: None
SEE: *Illustration 416.*

K.
Virga, Fortune, Kim, Doll Bodies, Grant Plastics, Niresk, Plastic Molded Arts, Norma, Ginny-Type Walking Dolls: all HP.

It is difficult to identify these dolls as belonging to a specific company without a box. However, there are differences in the quality of the dolls. For the most part Virga, Fortune, Kim and Norma made dolls of better quality.
SEE: *Illustration 417.*

K.
Virga, Fortune, Kim, Doll Bodies, Grant Plastics, Niresk, Plastic Molded Arts, Roberta Ginny-Type Walking Dolls: HP with vinyl head.
MARKS: None
SEE: *Illustration 418. Patricia Arches Collection.*

415.

416.

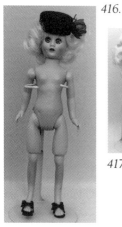

417.

418.

L.

1. *Vogue Painted-Eye Early HP Doll:* 8in (20cm); painted eyelashes top and to side of eye; non-walker; jointed at neck, shoulders and hips; 3rd and 4th fingers molded together; two lines at ankle; arm hook (see *Hard Plastic Dolls, I,* Identification Guide, page 267R); circa 1948-1950. Most of these dolls were not yet named *Ginny.*

MARKS: "Vogue" (head); "Vogue" (body)

SEE: *Illustration 419* (doll on left). *Pat Parton Collection.*

2. *Ginny:* HP; 8in (20cm); sleep eyes with painted eyelashes; heavy hard plastic; (see *Hard Plastic Dolls, I* for further general characteristics and *Illustration 556* for dressed doll); circa 1950-1953. A walking mechanism was added in 1954.

419.

The "poodle cut" wig was used only in 1952. This particular doll was the first one called *Ginny.* She is dressed in a black velvet skirt and organdy top and a straw hat. From this point on all of these small dolls made by Vogue were called *Ginny.*

MARKS: "Vogue" (head); "Vogue" (body)

SEE: *Illustration 419* (doll on right).

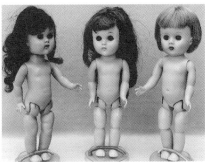

L.
Ginny: HP: 8in (20cm)   *420.*

3. All HP; pin-jointed straight-leg walker; sleep eyes with molded eyelashes; one line on ankle; other characteristics including arm hooks are the same; 1955-1956.

4. *All HP;* pin-jointed bent-knee walker; sleep eyes with molded eyelashes; other characteristics including arm hooks are the same; 1957-1962.

5. *HP body with vinyl head;* pin-jointed bent-knee walker; other characteristics including arm hooks are the same; the flesh tone of the plastic is very pink; quality of the vinyl in the head is excellent; 1963-1965.

MARKS: (Left to right) Dolls #1 and #2 "Ginny//Vogue Dolls//Inc.//(Pat. No 2687594)//Made in U.S.A." (body); "Vogue" (head); doll #3 the same except "Ginny" (head)

SEE: *Illustration 420.* Doll #3 *Phyllis Appel Collection;* Doll #5 *Barbara Comienski Collection.*

Comparison Chart of "Chubby-type" Dolls

The so-called "chubby" dolls, 10in (25cm) to 12in (31cm), have been favorites of children and collectors since the 1950s. They were really a large *Ginny*®-type doll that children could handle more easily. They had a large wardrobe that could be purchased where the dolls were sold. Each year new clothes were added to the line.

It is often very difficult to identify these dolls. Since they were usually sold in just panties, shoes and socks, very few of these dolls have original clothes. The clothing was purchased in boxes, and it is still possible to find some mint-in-box clothes for these dolls.

The chart below is an attempt to help collectors identify their dolls. It is not perfect, and there are many variations of each brand. In the end, these dolls may have come out of the same factory. There are differences in the quality of both the dolls and the clothes. There are even differences in the quality of the dolls within one company in any given year.

I. MARKS

A. Arranbee *Littlest Angel* (see page 55-62)
    1. "65" or "15" (vinyl head) often hard to read; "R & B" (waist)
    2. Inverted T (⊥) on *Surprise Doll* (vinyl head)
    3. "19" (vinyl head of doll with short, straight rooted hair)
    4. "R & B" 11 (vinyl head of doll with short, straight rooted hair)
    5. "R & B" (head of all-HP doll)
    6. "R & B" (head and back of all-HP doll)
    7. "R & B" (back only of all-HP doll)

B. Vogue *Li'l Imp* (see Hard Plastic Dolls I, page 257)
    1. "R & B//15" or "16" (vinyl head). It is often hard to read.
    2. "R & B//76" (vinyl head). It is often hard to read.
    3. "19" (vinyl-headed doll)

C. Block (see pages 69-70)
    1. No marks on all-HP *Baby Walker*
    2. "Block Doll Products" (vinyl-headed doll)

D. Nancy Ann *Debbie* all-HP "Nancy Ann" in raised letters (head)
    Nancy Ann *Debbie* vinyl head "Nancy Ann" (head)

E. Sayco *Miss America Pageant* doll
    1. "s" (vinyl head)
    2. "Sayco" (head)
    3. None

F. Togs and Dolls *Penny Walker*
    "Pat. Pending" (all HP body)

II. ARM HOOKS

A. Arranbee *Littlest Angel*
    1. All-HP dolls
    2. Hard plastic dolls with vinyl head
    3. *Japanese Surprise* doll with vinyl head.

B. Vogue *Li'l Imp* vinyl head
C. Block all-HP *Baby Walker* or vinyl-headed doll
D. Nancy Ann *Debbie* all-HP
E. Nancy Ann *Debbie* vinyl head
F. Sayco Miss America Pageant doll (vinyl head)

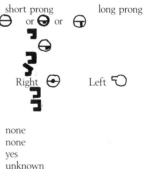

short prong   long prong

Right   Left

III. ELBOW DIMPLES

A. Arranbee *Littlest Angel* all-HP and vinyl head   none
B. Vogue *Li'l Imp* (vinyl head)   none
C. Block with *Baby Walker* all-HP   yes
    Block (vinyl head)   unknown
D. Nancy Ann *Debbie* all-HP and vinyl head   yes
E. Sayco *Miss America Pageant* doll (vinyl head)   yes (close together)

IV. WALKING MECHANISM AND LEGS

A. Arranbee *Littlest Angel*   hip-pin walker with jointed legs

B. Vogue *Li'l Imp* — hip-pin walker with jointed legs
C. Block all-HP *Penny Walker* — regular walking mechanism with straight legs

Block with vinyl head — regular walking mechanism with jointed knees
D. Nancy Ann *Debbie* all-HP — regular walking mechanism with straight legs

Nancy Ann *Debbie* with vinyl head — regular walker with jointed knees
E. Sayco *Miss America Pageant* doll with vinyl head — regular walker with jointed knees
F. Togs and Dolls *Penny Walker* all-HP — regular walker

V. MOUTH
A. Arrabnee *Littlest Angel* both all-HP and vinyl — Molded tongue in mouth
B. Vogue *Li'l Imp* vinyl head — Molded tongue in mouth
C. Block both all-HP and vinyl head — Closed mouth — no tongue
D. Nancy Ann *Debbie* all-HP and vinyl head — Closed mouth — no tongue
E. Sayco *Miss America Pageant* doll vinyl head — Closed mouth — no tongue
F. Togs and Dolls *Penny Walker* all-HP — Closed mouth — no tongue

VI. MOLDED HAIR UNDER WIG
A. Arranbee *Littlest Angel* all-HP — Sometimes
Arranbee *Littlest Angel* vinyl head — Usually no
Arranbee *Japanese Surprise* doll vinyl head — Molded hair under rooted hair
B. Vogue *Li'l Imp* vinyl head — No
C. Block *Baby Walker* all-HP — Yes
Block doll vinyl head — No
D. Nancy Ann *Debbie* all-HP — Yes
Nancy Ann *Debbie* vinyl head — No
E. Sayco *Miss America Pageant* doll vinyl head — No
F. Togs and Dolls *Penny Walker* all-HP — Yes

VII. PAINTED EYELASHES UNDER EYES
A. Arranbee *Littlest Angel* all-HP — wide spaced, short
Arranbee *Littlest Angel* vinyl head — wide spaced, short
B. Vogue *Li'l Imp* vinyl head — none
C. Block *Baby Walker* all-HP — dark paint
Block doll vinyl head — medium paint
D. Nancy Ann *Debbie* all-HP — long, dark paint
Nancy Ann *Debbie* vinyl head — wide spaced, medium paint
E. Sayco *Miss America Pageant* doll vinyl head — none
F. Togs and Dolls *Penny Walker* all-HP — unknown

VIII. POINTED NIPPLES ON BREASTS
A. Arranbee *Littlest Angel* all-HP — no
Arranbee *Littlest Angel* vinyl head — no
B. Vogue *Li'l Imp* vinyl head — no
C. Block *Baby Walker* all-HP — yes
D. Nancy Ann *Debbie* all-HP — unknown
Nancy Ann *Debbie* vinyl head — no
E. Sayco *Miss America Pageant* doll vinyl head — no
F. Togs and Dolls *Penny Walker* all-HP — yes

IX. STITCHING AROUND WIG NEAR NECKLINE
A. Arranbee *Littlest Angel* all-HP — no
Arranbee *Littlest Angel* vinyl head — no
B. Vogue *Li'l Imp* vinyl head — no
C. Block *Penny Walker* all-HP — yes
Block vinyl head — unknown
D. Nancy Ann *Debbie* all-HP — yes
Nancy Ann *Debbie* vinyl head — no
E. Sayco *Miss America Pageant* doll vinyl head — no
F. Togs and Dolls *Penny Walker* all-HP — no

Dress-Me Dolls

The following companies sold the "Dress-Me" type of doll. These were usually sold on a wholesale basis to companies which dressed dolls, doll supply shops, doll hospitals, craft shops and doll mail order companies.

1. Block Doll Creations
2. Central Toy Manufacturing Corporation
3. Commonwealth Plastics Corp.
4. Doll Bodies, Inc.
5. Grant Plastics
6. Reliable (Canada)
7. Rosebud (England)

Eyes

A.

Cosmopolitan Ginger Eyes (left to right):
1. Midwestern *Mary Jean* (large eyes)
2. Cosmopolitan *Ginger* (medium eyes)
3. Cosmopolitan *Ginger* (small eyes)

Many of the LARGE EYE dolls with *Ginger* characteristics seem to have been marketed by companies other than Cosmopolitan.

SEE: *Illustration 421.*

B.

Painted-Eye Ginger: HP; 8in (20cm); first *Ginger.*
MARKS: None
SEE: *Illustration 422. Pat Parton Collection.*

C.

Sarold (England) Ginny-type:* unusual unpainted molded eyebrows; (see *Illustration 342*, page 202). The Sarold Company made many small and inexpensive dolls. Most of them had this type of eyebrows. It is an excellent identification feature.

421.

422.

Fasteners
(Gripper Snaps)

Today the value of hard plastic dolls depends on the clothes that they are wearing. Collectors who have dolls without original clothes search for authentic costumes to increase the dolls' historical significance and value. For many years one of the methods of identification has been to look at the gripper snap fasteners.

In this section the doll collector can find a few examples of the fasteners used in the 1950s. This is just a start on this research, but perhaps the reader can use this section as a starting point for a study which will help locate original clothes.

A.
Cosmopolitan Ginger, Fortune Pam, Sayco Miss America Pageant Dolls fastener: the Cosmopolitan *Ginger* clothing is labeled; the Fortune *Pam* and Sayco *Miss America Pageant* clothing is not marked.
> **SEE:** *Illustration 423. Pat Parton Collection.*

B.
Nancy Ann Muffie and Debbie Snap Closings: two different types of gripper snap closings were used for both dolls. The first was a small snap with a solid top (right). The second was used later and was a snap with a double circle (left).
> **SEE:** *Illustration 424.*

C.
Nancy Ann Style Show Doll with Vinyl Head: the few dolls documented had the same small snap with the solid top (right). In these cases the snaps matched the color of the costume.
> **MARKS:** "Grippers S M C O" (second larger snap)
> **SEE:** *Illustration 424.*

D.
Ontario Plastics Paula Sue: unusual white gripper snap closing with several protrusions on top surface.
> **SEE:** *Illustration 425. Marge Meisinger Collection.*

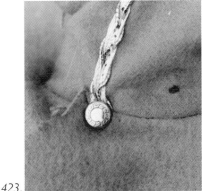
423.

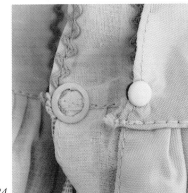
424.

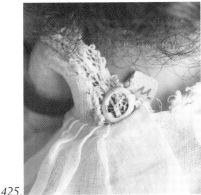
425.

E.

Vogue Fastener: type of gripper snap fastener usually found on clothes made by the Vogue Dolls, Inc.

Little Imp: "Starlet" on inside of snap.

Early Ginny: hook and eye closing.

SEE: *Illustration 426.*

426.

Foreign Dolls

Foreign dolls pictured in *Hard Plastic Dolls I*

Foreign Dolls Pictured in this Book

Hair Care Dolls

1. Arranbee: *Nanette, the Beauty Shop Doll* came with a beauty kit, curlers and easy instructions for doing hair; 1957; (see page 54).
2. Artisan: *Raving Beauty* advertised that she had Ravon hair that could be shampooed, combed and waved; 1950; (see page 63).
3. Baby Barry Toys: *Baby Barry* came with a "Wave-A-Doll Hair Kit;" (see page 67).
4. Effanbee: *Tintair Honey* came with hair dye, applicator and curlers; 1951; (see page 105).
5. Eugenia: *Perm-O-Wave Pam* came with plastic curlers, a make-up cape, barrette and carrying case; 1949 (see page 108).
6. Fleischaker Novelty Co.: *Little Girl of Today* came with human hair rooted in scalp. She had detailed hair styling instructions; 1951; (see page 111).
7. Fortune Toys, Incorporated: *Starlet the Lustercreme Shampoo* was an advertising doll; circa 1957; (see page 139).
8. Horsman: girl doll came with curlers, brush and comb set; early 1950s; (see page 124).
9. Ideal Toy Company: *Toni* came with a "Play Wave" kit; circa 1950-1955; (see *Hard Plastic Dolls, I*, page 144 and this book, page 135).
10. Pedigree (England): their *Toni*-type doll was almost identical with the Ideal *Toni* and came with a similar wave kit; circa 1953-55; (see page 185).

Rooted Hair in Hard Plastic Head

1. American Character: some *Sweet Sue* dolls have a skull cap with rooted hair glued onto the head; early 1950s; (see *Hard Plastic Dolls, I*, page 43).
2. Fleischaker: *Little Girl of Today* came with human hair rooted in the head; 1951; (see page 111).
3. Monica: *Marion* had hair rooted in hard plastic; circa 1953-55; (see *Hard Plastic Dolls, I*, page 181).
4. Unica (Belgium): HP girl doll has a rubber cap which is holding rooted hair; mid 1950s; (see page 209).

Colored Wigs on Dolls

During the 1950s women and children were experimenting with hair styles and color. It was becoming acceptable, and even fashionable, to have dyed hair. Dolls, especially the small walking dolls and larger ballerina dolls, often had pink, orange, blue, green and other colored hair. Children loved it. This is a partial list of dolls which could be purchased with brightly colored hair.

1. Admiration: *Ginny*·-type girl.
2. Cosmopolitan: *Ginger* with the large eyes.
3. Fortune: *Pam*.
4. Grant Plastics: *Suzie* and other small dolls
5. Virga: *Schapiarelli GoGo, Lollipop* and *Playmates*
6. Vogue: *Little Imp*.

Saucy Walker-type Dolls

Ideal's *Saucy Walker* and *Saucy Toddler* were very popular, well-made dolls in both boy and girl models. They were also expensive. Other companies, and Ideal itself, made cheaper versions which sold well. Some were marked with the competing company name but many were unmarked or with symbols like △ or AE. They were made of all-hard plastic or a combination of a hard plastic body and vinyl head.

The following companies competed with Ideal and made a *Saucy Walker*-type.

1. Aster Co.
2. Baby Barry: *Baby Barry*
3. Belle: *Playmate Walker* and *Heddi Stroller*
4. Doll-Land Division of Western Stationary Co.: *Angel Locks*
5. Eegee: *Susan Stroller* and *Merry Stroller*
6. P.J. Hill: *Cindy Walker*
7. Horsman: *Ruthie Walker*
8. Imperial: walking girl
9. Midwestern: *Suzy Stroller*
10. Natural: *Bride*
11. P & M: *Paula Mae*
12. Pedigree: walking boy and girl
13. Reliable: *Plassikin*
14. Roddy: boys and girls
15. Uneeda: *Country Girl*

Shoes and Feet

The hard plastic dolls can often be identified by their shoes and feet. The following pictures are in addition to those pictured in *Hard Plastic Dolls, I.*

The following is a reference list for those dolls pictured in *Hard Plastic Dolls, I.* The pages listed are all in *Hard Plastic Dolls, I.*

1. Molded feet from Plastic Molded Arts, A & H, Midwestern and Corrine Dolls (see page 283A).
2. Another type of feet used by Plastic Molded Arts, Peggy Huffman, Playhouse and others (see page 283B).
3. Mold-on PMA Indian (see page 283C).
4. Molded and painted shoe with bow used by A & H, Duchess, Lingerie Lou (Doll Bodies) and Grant Plastics (see page 284D).
5. Shoes used by Virga (Beehler Arts) and Fairyland Dolls (see page 284E).
6. Another molded shoe used by Virga (Beehler Arts) (see page 284F).
7. Fortune shoe with butterfly bow (see page 285G).
8. Another Fortune shoe with a thinner, upper roll (see page 285H).
9. Virga-Fortune and Duchess shoe (see page 285I).
10. Shoe used on dolls sold inexpensively such as Lovely (see page 286J).
11. Molded, painted Roberta shoe with bow (see page 286K).
12. Knickerbocker, S & E and Reliable of Canada (see page 286L).
13. Ideal plastic shoes (see page 286M).
14. A. & H. shoe with bow (see page 287N).
15. Ideal *Princess Mary* shoes (see page 287O).
16. Capezio ballerina shoes (see page 287P).

A.

American Character Sweet Sue Shoes: see *Illustrations 64* through *69* for a picture of an early *Sweet Sue* shoe from the 1952 catalog.

B.

Cosmopolitan Ginger Heel: unusual heel found on *Ginger* and *Ginger*-type dolls. An exception is the bent-knee doll (not pictured). This bent-knee doll has two different

characteristics that will help identify it:
1. Two lines above the ankle.
2. Unusual leg and ankle mold seam on the side of the leg.
    SEE: *Illustration 427.*

C.
Effanbee Shoes: see *Hard Plastic Dolls, I, Illustration 200* for a picture of the early *Honey Walker* simulated black patent leather slipper.

D.
Ideal Little Girl Shoes: There were two types of shoes made for Ideal little girl dolls during the hard plastic era. 1. Simulated leather with a snap in front. 2. Vinyl shoes with "Ideal" on the sole.

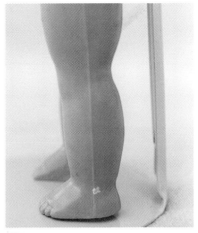

427.

The simulated leather shoes were shown in company catalogs through 1952. (See *Hard Plastic Dolls, I,* page 146. In this book see page 134.) Although some Ideal company advertisements showed these leather-like shoes in 1953, most of the dolls had vinyl shoes from then on through the hard plastic period.

The vinyl Ideal shoes are shown in *Hard Plastic Dolls, I,* page 286, *Illustration 625.* The flower design was only on a few of these vinyl shoes.

Baby and Toddler Shoes: The Ideal babies wore simple high-tie shoes of simulated leather. These can be seen in *Illustration 226.* A few of these high shoes have been seen on all-original *Toni* dolls.
Toni dolls.

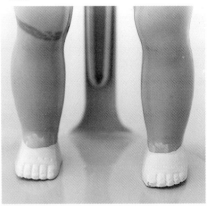

428.

E.
Midwestern Mary Jean: painted shoes showing toes; all other foot characteristics of the Cosmopolitan *Ginger* are the same.
    SEE: *Illustration 428.*

F.
Nancy Ann Muffie Shoes: There were two types of shoes; left is the earliest leather-like shoe with a small gripper snap closing; right is an all-plastic buckle shoe which was used on later dolls.
    SEE: *Illustration 429.*

429.

G.

Pedigree Small Walking Doll (Ginny-type): two different types of foot construction (see *Illustration 309*); doll on left has painted shoes and socks; doll on right has a regular foot with good toe detail.

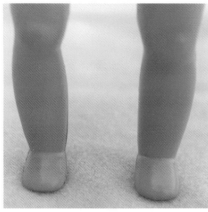

430.

H.

Uneeda Feet (Ginny-type) Doll: the feet on the 8in (20cm) walking doll shows no toe detail.

SEE: *Illustration 430.*

I.

Beehler Arts, Fortune, Virga Molded-on Slippers (Ginny-Type Dolls):
1. Doll on left is a Fortune *Pam.*
2. Doll on right is a Plastic Molded Arts *Joannie.*

Other dolls with the same molded slipper include Doll Bodies *Mary Lu:* Fortune *Ninette, Starlet;* Grant Plastics *Suzie;* Niresk *Joannie;* Norma *Norma;* Roberta *Jeannie;* Virga *Lucy, Playmates* and *Lolly-Pop.*

SEE: *Illustration 431.*

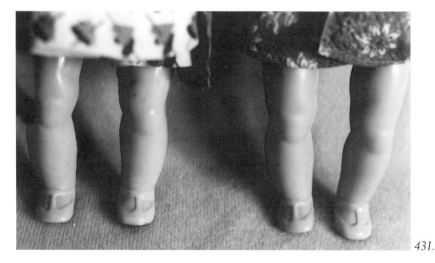

431.

Talking Dolls

1. Art-Doll Creations (English)
2. Joy Toys, Inc. (dolls talk in English, Spanish, French and Portuguese)
3. Pedigree (English)

INDEX

Hard Plastic Dolls — Vol. I: Price Updates

Many of the prices of individual dolls found in *Hard Plastic Dolls I* have been updated in *Hard Plastic Dolls II*. A list of prices for those dolls not pictured in *Hard Plastic Dolls II* are listed below. If the illustration number of a doll in *Hard Plastic Dolls I* is not shown, please check the company prices in this book.

Illustration	Page	Price
Ill. 3	11	$ 8-12
Ill. 4	11	12-18
Ill. 5	11	15-30
Ill. 6	12	10-14
Ill. 7, 8	13	7-9
Ill. 9	13	30-35 each
Ill. 10, 11	14	20-25
Ill. 13-16	16, 17	8-12
Ill. 17	18	100-125 HP
Ill. 19	18	75-90 with vinyl head
Ill. 21	20	300-400
Ill. 22	20	450-500
Ill. 23	20	600-650
Ill. 24	20	250-350
Ill. 25	20	400-475
Ill. 26	21	600-700
Ill. 27	21	500-600
Ill. 28	21	600-700
Ill. 30	21	225-325
Ill. 34	22	475-525
Ill. 35	22	325-375 less if dress has faded
Ill. 36	22	400-500
Ill. 41-43	24	250-325
Ill. 45-49	25	250-800*
Ill. 50	26	800-1000
Ill. 53	26	500-600
Ill. 54-63	27, 28	200-1400*
Ill. 64-66	29	300-650*
Ill. 67-69	30-31	350-500+*
Ill. 70-74	32	300-325 each
Ill. 75	33	450-550
Ill. 76	33	950-1100
Ill. 77	34	375-450
Ill. 78	35	300-350
Ill. 79	35	250-325
Ill. 80	35	250-325
Ill. 81	36	650-750
Ill. 82	36	225-275
Ill. 83, 84	37	400-500
Ill. 85	38	450-550
Ill. 86	38	400-500
Ill. 87	39	400-500 up
Ill. 88	40	475-525
Ill. 89, 90	40	200-250
Ill. 91	41	100-125
Ill. 92	42	100-150
Ill. 94	43	65-85
Ill. 137	58	20-25
Ill. 138	59	300-350
Ill. 139	59	375-475
Ill. 140	60	300-325
Ill. 141-143	61, 62	275-325
Ill. 145	63	400-450
Ill. 146	64	100-135
Ill. 147, 148	65	145-150
Ill. 149, 151	66	50-75
Ill. 150	66	40-50
Ill. 153	66	175-225
Ill. 152, 154, 155	67, 68	135-150
Ill. 156	68	60-75
Ill. 157	69	350-400
Ill. 158	69	140-170
Ill. 159	69	35-50
Ill. 160	70	40-50
Ill. 161	70	200-250
Ill. 162	71	20-22
Ill. 163-165	71	50-75
Ill. 166	73	50-75
Ill. 167	73	125-150
Ill. 168, 169	75	50-150*
Ill. 171	76	50-75
Ill. 172	76	35-50
Ill. 173	77	30-35
Ill. 175, 177	78	15-20
Ill. 178	79	15-20
Ill. 179, 180	80	15-18
Ill. 181, 182, 185	81, 82	35-55+
Ill. 183, 184	82	100-120+
Ill. 186	82	40-55
Ill. 187-189	83, 84	8-15
Ill. 190	84	18-25
Ill. 192-196	85-86	20-25
Ill. 197	87	70-80
Ill. 198, 199	87	35-40
Ill. 205	90	120-140
Ill. 206-209	91	120-130
Ill. 210-213	92	250-300
Ill. 214-217	93	80-100
Ill. 218	94	125-150
Ill. 219	96	8-11
Ill. 220	97	150-175
Ill. 223, 224	98	12-18
Ill. 226, 228	99	90-150
Ill. 229, 230	100	125-150 up
Ill. 231	100	50-75
Ill. 232	100	80-90
Ill. 233, 234	101	30-70*
Ill. 235	102	40-50
Ill. 237, 238	103	35-40
Ill. 239	103	15-20
Ill. 240	103	20-27
Ill. 244	104	35-40
Ill. 245	105	8-10
Ill. 246	105	25-35
Ill. 247-253	107-109	60-150*
Ill. 254	109	125-160
Ill. 255, 258	109, 110	50-60
Ill. 264-271	113-114	15-20
Ill. 272	115	450-500
Ill. 273	116	175-225

*depending on costume

**working condition

Continued

256